GARDENING
IN THE SHADE

GARDENING
IN THE SHADE

MARGERY FISH

CAPITAL BOOKS INC.

First published 1964
By W. H. and L. Collingridge Limited
Reissued 1972
By David and Charles (publishers) Limited
And by Readers Union Limited
First published as a paperback 1983
By Faber and Faber Limited
Reissued in paperback 2000
By B.T. Batsford
9 Blenheim Court
Brewery Road
London N7 9NT

© Lesley Boyd-Carpenter 2000
The right of Margery Fish to be identified as the author and illustrator of this work has been
asserted by her estate in accordance with the Copyright, Designs and Patents Act 1988
© Foreword by Graham Rice 2000

Printed and bound by
The Cromwell Press, Trowbridge, Wiltshire.

A catalogue record for this book is available from the British Library.

ISBN 0 7134 8560 4

ISBN 1-892123-26-6

Capital Books Inc.
22841 Quicksilver Drive
Sterling, Virginia 20166

Contents

Acknowledgements

Grateful acknowledgement is made to Andrew Norton for taking most of the pictures in this edition and for his permission to reproduce them. Kind thanks also to Jack Keogh and the East Lambrook Manor Garden Slide Library, who supplied the remainder of the pictures.

Foreword

Gardeners everywhere worry about which plants will thrive in the shadier parts of their gardens. So the first and most fundamental revelation that shines through *Gardening in the Shade* is that a shady garden or a shady border is not a problem, it's an opportunity; shade is a place to grow and enjoy the many plants for which shade is their natural home.

Even after this basic message has sunk in, many gardeners limit their choice of shade plants to the familiar and popular shade-lovers, such as hostas, ferns and hellebores. Margery Fish does not stop there. Ever keen to try new species and cultivars and to assess which plants may unexpectedly thrive in shade, Mrs Fish delights and surprises us in this book by revealing the range and variety of plants she grew successfully in the shade at her garden at East Lambrook Manor in Somerset – plants that we can grow too.

When Margery Fish published this book in 1964 the pre-occupation with trying new plants was considerably less than it is now. Today, any plant claimed to be new is the instant target of collector-gardeners irrespective of the plant's intrinsic qualities. Mrs Fish grew new species introduced from the wild by plant hunters, new cultivars sent to her by friends, and had an unrivalled eye for variants that appeared in her garden and in those of her friends. She tried and assessed them, discarded some and grew those that seemed to her both good and distinct.

In fact her eye for subtle variation causes problems for both today's gardener and plant taxonomist as details that she identified and used to distinguish one form from another sometimes either elude or fail to match those now setting the standards for plant names (see 'Plant-name changes' at the back of the book).

Gardening in the Shade is an exciting book; it's full of insight into the problems and advantages of garden shade; full of ideas for plants to grow there; and has an inclusive feel that encourages gardeners to believe that they can make the shady areas of their gardens both interesting and beautiful.

Graham Rice
February 2000

Introduction

Some people think that to own a shady garden should be a matter for sympathy, but I always feel it is one for envy. Anyone with a garden without shade knows how difficult it is to grow many plants, for you cannot make shade overnight, but it is usually possible to contrive sunny spots in the shadiest garden.

Trees are the making of a good garden; they give grace and beauty and a feeling of stability. If I had to choose between a sunny and a shady garden I would choose the shady one every time, not only for its peace and timelessness but also for the plants that can be grown in it. It seems to me that they are often more interesting and more beautiful than those that like to bask in the sun.

Then there is the mystery. The gardens that are remembered are those that lure you on. No one wants to linger in a garden that has no surprises and if the whole garden can be seen at once there is a tendency to pay less attention to its treasures than if they were discovered in unexpected places under trees, behind walls and round corners.

Gardening in the shade can be more of a challenge than in a straightforward sunny garden. It may be necessary to take more trouble but it can have many surprises, for there are many plants usually grown in sun that will do quite well in shade. No one can tell until they have tried, so there is the great interest of experiment and the thrill of success.

There is an idea that shady gardens are dark and dull, but they need not be. Many plants with light, variegated or golden foliage will lighten dark places. Shades of green, varying textures of leaf and bark, and unusual shapes all help to break up the density of shade, even the silken seed-heads of some of the clematis bring light and life to a difficult corner.

There are, of course, many degrees of shade. The deep shade of trees varies and in some cases is accompanied by soil impoverished by hungry roots. Not many things will grow under beeches, but how lovely is an uninterrupted carpet of silvery moss, making a change from plants. Elms have roots that wander far afield and though hungry do not discourage the most determined weeds, but ivy is often found growing at the base of these trees, so cultivated ivies and shrubs that like the same conditions will sometimes succeed. The dappled shade from trees that are not too big or too thickly planted is perfect for rhododendrons and other woodland shrubs and plants, and practically anything will grow in the light shade cast by walls and buildings, shrubs and tall perennials.

Soil is most important and more trouble is necessary to improve soil in a shady garden than is normally necessary, for tree roots steal the nourishment, walls keep off the rain and the airless conditions of neglected shrubberies mean dank and lifeless soil. All this must be remedied and greater attention to adequate watering is necessary. Mulching, too, plays a greater part in gardens that are liable to dry out. Chopped bracken, leaf-mould, compost or spent hops are all helpful and should be used freely.

Gardening changes with the times and I think today's gardens will be remembered for the more general use of trees and shrubs and their informal association with many less usual plants which are happiest in shade.

~ 1 ~

The Importance of Soil

The reason why many people fail to grow good plants in shade is, I think, that not enough trouble is taken with the soil.

Not only is the soil under trees impoverished, but lack of moisture and nourishment also applies to beds under high walls. Walls do not suck moisture from the soil, as trees do, but they keep off the rain and there is no kindly benefice of fallen leaves to improve the soil. Nature's gift of leaves can replenish much of the nourishment taken out by growing plants, so I always make a point of giving beds under walls a particularly generous largesse of manure or compost.

There are two schools of thought about the leaves that fall. Some people let them lie and this is the best thing to do if nothing else is being done to the beds. I usually collect them and make them into compost because nature's scheme sometimes goes awry when the leaves fall in the wrong place or are whipped away by strong winds. And in gardens where slugs and snails are particularly troublesome they can do a lot of damage under the leaves without anyone realising it. If there is time I think it is a good idea to collect up all the leaves and use them as compost or leaf-mould, which is spread methodically over the whole garden each autumn.

Everyone has their own system of compost-making, and the size of the garden governs the system used. I have enough room to make a big heap and after many years of doing it the whole system of composting follows a regular routine. At first it was rather hit and miss, but when I knew what was wanted I hedged a long narrow enclosure with *Lonicera nitida*, and concreted it for easier working. The enclosure is at the top of the ditch so the concrete has a very slight tilt that way, and all round the edge, under the hedges, are gullies which catch the liquid and drain it through pipes under the hedge into containers. This gives me a source of liquid manure to be diluted and used on plants coming into flower or needing an extra fillip.

My heap is made from instructions in an American book called *Pay Dirt* which I read many years ago and it seems to work well with me, although some gardeners might find other ingredients more suitable for their soils.

All through the year we empty our barrows and trugs of annual weeds, decaying vegetation and everything cut from herbaceous plants to make a heap at one end of the enclosure. Grass cuttings and all kitchen waste go on this heap but evergreen cuttings and loppings are buried in the ditch we are filling up in the orchard, and diseased plants and bad weeds are burnt.

Every year in late autumn we wheel away the large heap of compost that has been standing for a year. I am often asked where I find room to put it in a garden that is so thickly planted as mine but I do try to leave as much clear soil as I can for this exercise, and if there is not much room it is put in small heaps where there is room and then forked into small morsels to be distributed evenly over the whole bed. I do not pretend it does not take time, and many people could not possibly do it; I am always quite relieved when we have finished the job and got the new lot before bad weather stops us. A good man can do it in my garden in about four days, and I finish off the detail spreading at my leisure.

I try to keep the new heap as flat and rectangular as possible as there is always a tendency to make each layer smaller until one has a pointed rick in the end instead of a completely flat rectangular heap. I get some farm manure each year as I let my orchard to a farmer, and another piece of land is let to a chicken farmer who sells me the peat litter from the chicken houses.

First we make a 6-in layer of the decayed greenstuff, then comes a layer of farmyard manure which is covered with chicken peat (light soil could be used instead), and a thin layer of wood ash goes on top of this. I have four short metal drainpipes which are placed vertically at intervals down the heap and lifted as more material is spread. We continue the layers until all the material is used and I often tip more wood ash on top later on if I have not time to use it elsewhere. One year we made a very neat heap because we had lifted some turf and the turves were used upside down all round the edge of the top layer.

Most people, of course, have not time or room to make compost that takes two years to mature and in hungry gardens every little bit of compost is needed the moment it is made. Small heaps can be made and enclosed by boards or wire-netting and treated regularly with an activator. They need plenty of moisture and must be watered in dry weather, and often need turning, this depending on the system used.

I used to make leaf-mould by collecting oak and beech leaves and though this is very good stuff for woodland plants, primroses and such plants it does take a very long time to rot down sufficiently to be used, and means yet another heap. I had to leave it at least two years before it was fit to use and sometimes wondered if I did not occasionally introduce such horrors as woodlice and vine weevils in greater numbers than I normally get. Now I put the leaves into the compost as a matter of expediency. I may get pests in the compost but I also get plenty of nice pink worms, which I was warned I might not have if I made compost on cement instead of soil.

Planting in our garden follows a regular pattern. Everything in the way of a shrub or tree gets a very big hole with some decayed farmyard manure incorporated in the soil below the line of the roots, and all smaller plants are put in with sand and peat added to the heavy clay soil. The bucket of sand and peat is particularly necessary when dividing plants, but nearly everything settles in better when it is used. In spite of trying to improve my soil for more than twenty years there are still parts which are nothing but pure, weeping clay, and when I have trays of soil in which seeds have been grown or cuttings taken I dig out as much of the clay as I can and fill in with the good potting compost. The clay goes to fill in the ditch in the orchard.

Many gardeners are not lucky enough to have farmyard manure and then chemical substitutes are good. For bulbs and such things that do not like manure, bonemeal is excellent because its goodness lasts and is absorbed by the soil over a long period. Dried blood and hoof and horn work in the same way and are excellent when the soil is poor.

Humus can be added to the soil by using it first as a mulch in dry weather and then incorporating it with the soil. I have seen several gardens where a thick layer of straw is spread on the soil among raspberries, vegetables and other utility crops where the farmyard look does not matter. In the flower or shrub garden one can use grass cuttings (which are allowed to cool before being used), chopped bracken or spent hops. Hop manure or seaweed are good or even chopped nettles, and for places where it doesn't show too much, sludge or shoddy.

Burnt soil has excellent properties and has a most stimulating effect on hellebores, peonies and other hungry subjects. If one has areas infested with difficult perennial weeds, even plants that are a nuisance, the soil can be dug out and burnt. This is the only way I can get rid of the brittle white roots of enchanter's nightshade, and *Campanula rapunculoides*, and it is possible to clear small areas of bindweed couch grass and butterbur in the same way, but of course it is a big operation for any but small gardens.

Not only is it necessary to feed the soil, it should be kept aerated, especially heavy soil. Never leave footmarks on the beds, as they cause the soil to become sour, and the soil under trees and in shady beds among shrubs should be lightly forked whenever it becomes hard. If a crust forms the air cannot get in, nor rain when it descends, and of course the constant harassing of the soil does make life more unpleasant for the weeds.

All gardens are better if they are worked regularly and peat or humus added when the soil is poor, and it is essential in a garden that is shady.

~ 2 ~

A Shady Border

Spring and Early Summer

There are certain advantages about a shady border which do not apply to a border made in full sun. The most important is that it makes it far easier to have a planting that is colourful and interesting all through the year. Many of the plants that flower early in the year do best in shade and cannot therefore be used in the average sunny border.

The hellebores, for instance, need a shady site with a rich, humus-laden soil and in most gardens have to be planted under trees or in odd shady corners. But if the border is shady they can be included to give life to the border in the winter and being mostly evergreen their leaves will help throughout the year.

The two species that flower earliest are *H. olympicus** and *H. atrorubens**. *H. olympicus** has flowers of greenish white and they are often out as early as October, and go on well into the New Year. Late November and early December sees the first plum-purple flowers of *H. atrorubens** opening at ground level without any leaves. As the stalks grow more flowers open until there is a normal perfectly balanced plant about the turn of the year, and it will remain for a month or more. Another early variety is *H. orientalis (kochii)**, which has rather flat flowers in greenish white and blooms very profusely. The unopened flowers crowd thickly on the ground in early December and are sometimes open before Christmas. All the forms of *H. orientalis* can be used for they are all lovely and have no objection to hobnobbing with other plants so long as they are not disturbed and are kept moist and well fed.

The Christmas Rose, *H. niger*, dislikes disturbance more than any of them, but is lovely when in full flower and too good to be hidden in a part of the garden seldom seen. *H. n. altifolius (maximus)** is the earliest and has large pink-flushed flowers on long stalks. *H.* 'Potters Wheel' is a recent introduction and one of the most beautiful, with very large pure white flowers which sometimes open before Christmas. *H. foetidus* and *H. corsicus**, with their green flowers and handsome foliage, start to flower in December and go on for several months.

Early colour will come from pulmonarias, for the first can be seen blooming in December; in fact, *P. rubra* is often called the Christmas Cowslip. It is a bright brick-pink and very exciting to find on a cold winter's day. Normally the foliage is rather light green and unspotted although there is a form attributed to the late E.

A. Bowles, on whose shoulders so much garden fame has descended, which has spotted leaves. The various forms of *P. officinalis*, with their little blue and pink flowers, come next and are not deterred by weather. I have brushed snow off them and found them quite undamaged. The dazzling blue pulmonaria,
P. angustifolia, is the last to flower, usually before its green leaves, and is as blue as an anchusa. The large spotted leaves of pulmonaria are attractive early in the year but they get large and coarse by mid-season and are best planted at the back of the border where they can melt into the herbage.

Two other early-flowering subjects can be planted well back too, although their foliage is never unattractive. The large yellow daisies of doronicum are welcome in early spring and are tempered by the bright green of their leaves.   *D. austriacum* is about 1 ½ ft high; several others, including the fairly new *D.* 'Miss Mason', are about 2 to 3 ft. The friend who gave me *Hacquetia* (*Dondia*) *epipactis* had no idea of its name and I had to wait until early spring the next year to discover what an exciting plant it is. The first inkling of its presence comes from little greeny gold flowers that open at ground level and have glistening green petals rather like a buttercup and large centres composed of tiny yellow flowers. As the stems grow more flowers open and later the leaves, which are a cross between a buttercup and a hellebore, grow to 6 to 8 in.

Bulbs are useful to give colour in the early months and primroses and polyanthus will be very happy. I always feel so sorry for these woodland plants when they are planted in full sun, and it is sad to see them bent double on a warm spring day. I grow many of my primroses, doubles, jacks-in-the-green and singles, as well as polyanthus, in the shade of tall perennials, and they do well because these plants do not steal so much from the soil as some shrubs and trees. Tall primulas such as denticulata and the candelabra types will grow quite well in a shady border because shade enables them to do so without so much moisture.

In April the lovely pink and white flowers of *Dicentra spectabilis* swing gracefully from arching stems, and remain perfect for several weeks. Like the hellebores this plant does not like disturbance. With roots as brittle as glass great damage can be done with an intruding fork. The dwarf forms flower a little later.

More use could be made of aquilegias; they flower early in the year, take up little room and give a light touch among heavier subjects. In April the short spurred *A. alpina*, growing from 9 to 12 in, starts to flower and from then on there are many from which to choose. The darker blue 'Hensoll Harebell' is a form of *A. alpina* and grows a little taller. It is profligate with its children, which come in varying shades of blue. I wish *A. vulgaris nivea* (*A.* 'Munstead White')* would be as generous. It has pale green leaves and was one of Miss Gertrude Jekyll's favourites. I have a red-flowered aquilegia, *A. coccinea**, which grows rather tall but has so many of its small red flowers that they do not look out of proportion. It came from a pinch of seed pressed on me by a friend and I am glad that this time my seed-sowing was more successful than usual. I also like a striking red and yellow aquilegia, *A. canadensis*, which is sturdy and not as tall as most of the others but has exceptionally big flowers. The clematiflora hybrids have clematis-shaped flowers in many shades of pink and blue. The pale blue *A. caerulea* looks lovely with the soft pink Rose Queen, with the crimson and white Crimson Star to add depth. I still think the short-spurred varieties have great charm but the modern trend is to develop spurs as long as possible. In the pale yellow *A. longissima* the spurs reach 6 in and the spurs in 'Mrs Scott Elliott's Strain' and the 'McKana Hybrids' are exceptionally long.

I try to keep purple linaria in walls and in the beds outside the garden where its blue-green foliage and spikes of small purple flowers make a pleasant change, but it seeds prolifically and it is constant war. The soft pink *Linaria* 'Canon J. Went'* seeds itself too but it gets a better reception; it is scented of honey and I let many of its numerous children remain.

Though heucheras are usually planted in sun the heucherellas seem to do best in shade, *H*. 'Bridget Bloom' certainly does. It is a lovely plant with its tapering spires of shell-pink flowers and light green leaves. *H*. x *tiarelloides** is a much more robust plant and increases better for me. It has larger, deeper flowers and the bright green basal leaves are bigger, well pencilled and with a faint pink tinge in early growth. *Tellima grandiflora* is of course a good plant for shade and increases well. I wish *H. rubescens* would do as well. This is a lovely plant for the front of a shady border. Its early leaves are a soft pink and later become a dark purplish crimson. The flowers, unlike the tall green spikes of tellima, are rather small and not very distinct in colour. I think greenish buff would describe them best, but it is not for the flowers that one grows this plant. *H. viridis* has flowers very similar to those of tellima, but the green does not fade to pink and the leaves of the plant, though a handsome dark green, have no markings and no shades of pink when they are very young.

A geum that grows well in shade and starts to flower in April and continues for much of the year is *G. rivale* 'Leonard's variety'. The flowers are quite large, rosy salmon on the outside and glowing orange within.

No family gives us more ideas for the shady border than the campanulas. Of the many suitable quite a number flower on and off for months on end. The various forms of *C. persicifolia* do, and they seed themselves about the garden, often furnishing odd corners that would otherwise be dull. I am quite satisfied with the ordinary varieties of the peach-leaved bellflower, but there are named varieties to be had which are said to have larger and better-coloured flowers.

C. p. 'Telham Beauty' has extra large flowers of deep blue, *C. p.* 'Wirral Belle' and 'Bluebell' are also deep in colour. In *C. p.* 'Beechwood' the flowers are paler and *C. p.* 'Cantab' is the bright Cambridge blue one would expect, and *C. p.* 'Snowdrift' is the named variety of white *C. persicifolia. C. p.* 'Pride of Exmouth' is a double blue form, and the double white, which looks rather like a gardenia is *C. p.* 'Fleur de Neige', but not as easy as some of them.

Usually white flowers are less robust than the coloured forms but not with these campanulas. I have at least half a dozen cup-and-saucer forms of this campanula in white. They seed themselves, some have touches of green, others are flat, but all are strong growing and increase well. So far I have been able to find only one in blue, and that in a rather pale washy blue and without much stamina. I feel there must be a better blue somewhere with darker flowers and a stronger constitution.

It is a pity that *C. glomerata* is such a wanderer. Its rich deep blue is not at all a common colour and to get a flower as big as the clustered bellflower is helpful in any colour scheme, but one's enthusiasm is tempered when it takes over from less rampant plants and works its fleshy roots farther and farther afield. I have been given one which I am told does not spread but so far I have not had time to be sure. The garden form of *C. glomerata* is *C. g. dahurica**, and *C. g. d.* 'Joan Elliott' is an improved form, very deep in colour, slightly earlier and a good cut flower, while *C. g. superba** is the tallest, growing to 2 ½ ft. The dwarf form, *C. g. acaulis** (*nana*) is 6 in only. The white *C. glomerata alba** is very beautiful, only 1 ½ ft high and with the sturdy good temper of all these campanulas.

There is a little confusion in the minds of the uninitiated between *C. lactiflora, C. latifolia* and *C. latiloba.* It is easy to remember *C. lactiflora* because the flowers are the very pale blue of watered milk. It seeds itself freely and usually in awkward places and some of the seedlings are practically white. There is a deeper coloured form in *C. l.* 'Pritchard's var', and a pale lilac-pink *C. l.* 'Loddon Anna'. Why the people who dislike staking do not make more use of the dwarf *C. l.* 'Pouffe' I do not know. The neat 9-in mounds are ideal front-of-the-border plants and do not get out of hand.

C. latifolia is a strong fleshy plant with stout stems rising from a neat basal rosette. The flowers are large and urn-shaped and hang from the stems. It has forms in white and blue, and the named varieties are *C. l.* 'Brantwood', a good dark blue, and 'Miss Willmot's white'. I have *C. l. macrantha** growing very contentedly in the shade of *Angelica archangelica* in my garden.

C. latiloba is a favourite old bellflower of our grandmothers, with 3- to 4-ft spikes of large open flowers packed tight against the stems. The ordinary white and blue forms are still excellent plants for dry shade and have thick evergreen foliage which is valuable as ground cover for awkward places. This campanula sometimes appears in lists as *C. grandis** and the two named varieties *C. l.* 'Highcliffe' and *C. l.* 'Percy Piper', both 3 ft, have larger, deeper blue flowers.

There are three good campanulas with large hanging bells which seem out of proportion to the 2-ft stems, and I find *C. burghaltii** the best. It always surprises me that such a good plant is so easy to grow. It wants to co-operate and increases well without ramping so is very easy to propagate. The flowers are a pale slaty blue with deeper buds, such soft colour is good for relief. It starts to flower in June and is still at it in November and I find it difficult to understand why so few nurseries list it. *C.* x *van houttei** is very similar in colour and habit, although darker, but not nearly such an easy plant to please. I had it in several places in the garden and I think all have disappeared. It did not increase for me and flowered only once in June. *C. punctata* is not often grown either, but it does increase well by wandering about underground and has large cream or pink bells on rather stumpy stems. It gets its name from the crimson spots inside the bells and definitely does better in shade.

I am very fond of *C. alliariifolia*, and though it was given to me in the first place as *C. allionii* I was then too ignorant to know that I was getting a commoner instead of an aristocrat. Now I am glad because *C. alliariifolia* is still with me and I am sure *C. allionii* would not be. I like its hairy heart-shaped leaves and long spires of hanging cream bells which get smaller as they climb. It will stand a lot of shade, will keep itself in the picture with an occasional seedling and goes on blooming until December.

The tall *C. pyramidalis*, known as the Chimney Bellflower, is best treated as a biennial, and it is often grown as a pot plant for the cold greenhouse, not because it is tender but dating from the Victorian custom of filling the conservatory leading out of the dining room or drawing room with colourful long-blooming plants. For years I had healthy plants sprouting from my walls, where they always seemed very insecure with such long and heavily loaded stems growing from a tiny crevice. I suppose in the end the wind destroyed them before they had time to flower. The hybrid of *C. pyramidalis* and *C. versicolor*, known as *C.* x *pyraversii*, is 2 ft only and more likely to survive bad weather.

The nettle-leaved bellflowers, *C. trachelium*, are shade lovers and attractive over a long period. They grow to about 2 ft and make neat, upright plants. The only named variety I know is *C. t.* 'Bernice', which has double powder-blue flowers, there is also a single blue, a single white and a double white. They do not spread and need careful propagation by division or cuttings.

Only the completely wild parts of the garden are suitable for *C. rapunculoides*, which is one of the worst runners I know. It got into my garden under a false name, *Adenophera potanini**, and I had no idea when I bought it that I should never be able to get rid of it. Digging it out just encourages it to double the efforts of the bits that are left. I take out barrowloads of soil in which it is growing and then burn it but unless I take up stone paths, a sundial and stone edgings the hide-and-seek game will go on. But I should enjoy this campanula if I had a really wild place for it, for its flowers are most attractive and very good to pick. Those long and graceful wands of graduated blue bells have helped me out in the house many a time and if one could contrive a home for it in a narrow bed between a wall and a stone path it could not get up to much mischief.

At first glance one would take *Symphyandra hofmannii* for a campanula. It has hanging bell-shaped flowers in cream and has the growth of a canterbury bell and the habit. Although it is a perennial it is not a long-lived one but after seeing the way it was seeding itself under the trees in a friend's garden I thought it would do the same for me, but it hasn't so far. I am giving it another chance when I hope it will seed as generously as the biennial *Verbascum blattaria*, with its tall spires of white or yellow flowers, which grows well in shade and has neat dark green rosettes. There is another symphyandra, *S. pendula*, which has weeping funnel-shaped flowers. Platycodons are a little higher in the social register than campanulas and gardeners who might not admit the more ordinary campanulas will always find room for the balloon flowers. One reason why they are not common may be that they disappear completely after flowering and don't show any sign of growth until April, so that if they are not marked it is easy for their roots to be damaged.

There is an irresistible temptation to children—and others—to burst the flat balloon-like buds before they open, for the point where the petals are joined asks for the pressure of a thumb. The tallest is *P. grandiflorus*, 1 ½ ft high in blue, white, pink or semi-double, with *P. g. maresii* about a foot. There is now a real dwarf, for *P. g. apoyama** is 3 in only. It has violet-blue flowers and is a gem for the front of the border or the shady rock garden.

Delphiniums are best in sun. They grow too tall in shade, although it doesn't affect their flowering. I put the double delphinium in the shade of apple trees and it flowered extremely well although the spikes reach 4 to 5 ft instead of the customary 3 ft. The dwarf delphiniums listed under belladonna hybrids* would not grow so tall and the 1 ½ ft *D. tatsienense*, with gentian-blue flowers, will flower in shade. The grandiflorum delphiniums, although they are perennial, are usually grown from seed every year and used like bedding plants. Azure Fairy in bright Cambridge blue is probably the most popular but there are also varieties in lavender, deep blue and white, and they can all be grown in light shade. Care must be taken to keep them from being eaten to the ground by slugs. The Tibetan delphinium does best in shade and is different from most delphiniums. It makes a fairly bushy clump with leaves on slender stems and its dark blue flowers grow on wiry arching stems. I grow it in a pocket between stones in my ditch garden, so that the flowers can grow naturally. Slugs love the new growth of all delphiniums, so special care has to be taken in the early stages, particularly in shady gardens where slugs and snails abound.

In late spring we welcome the soft lavenders and creams of the thalictrums. *T. aquilegiifolium* is one of the most charming; it is extremely easy and accommodating and I often wonder that it is not grown more widely. It has large fluffy heads in varying shades of lavender, cream or white, they last for several weeks and often come at a time when there is a lull between flowers. Even if it did not flower the plant would be worth growing for its smooth grey-green foliage, which is like that of a columbine. This thalictrum grows to about 3 ft and seeds itself quite freely but I have never had seedlings from the smaller one, called 'Dwarf Purple', which has darker purple heads on 2-ft stems.

There are places, particularly in a shady garden, where the 'maiden hair plant', *T. minus** (*T. adiantifolium*), can be introduced. It is very pretty with most delicate ferny foliage and small green flowers, all good for picking. But for all its fragility it has a will of iron and its fine yellow roots are as tough as wire. I do grow it in a shady border and also on top of a wall under a beech hedge, but I don't plant it next to plants that aren't strong enough to stand up for themselves and I am always removing the shoots that stray too far from the fold. I have been given a form which is said not to be invasive and so far it has lived up to its recommendation. This thalictrum turns a rich gold in autumn and is very dramatic posed against darker foliage.

The taller types flower later and can be divided into two groups, those with yellow flowers and the others with lavender and white flowers. The tallest of the yellows is *T. speciosissimum* (*glaucum*)* which grows to 5 ft and more. *T. s.* 'Illuminator' has variable green and yellow foliage and in *T. s. sphaerocephalum* the flower-heads are rounded instead of being flat. *T. speciosissimum** is my favourite, for its blue foliage is beautiful long after the fluffy lemon flowers are over.

The flowers of *T. dipterocarpum** vary slightly, some having more white stamens in proportion to the lilac sepals that cover them. Well-grown plants can have 2-ft heads of flowers on branching sprays a foot across, and grown in light shade against a dark background the effect is very pleasing. To get the best results plant fairly deeply in rich soil. The white form seldom grows more than 3 ft, and is very lovely with tiny pale green leaves. The deep purple *T. d.* 'Hewitt's Double' will grow to 5 ft in the right position, and its perfect double flowers, which are tiny and quite round, last for several weeks.

There is an interesting thalictrum recently introduced from Tibet and not yet very widely circulated. *T. diffusiflorum* has flowers about three times as large as any of the others, in a good lilac. The foliage is grey-green and very finely cut and the plants I have seen have not been more than a foot in height although I believe they are sometimes about twice this height.

It is sometimes difficult to decide which shade plants are best in a border or in the less formal woodland parts of the garden. I think one has more license when the garden is shady and it does not matter how informal the material and the planting so long as it is designed to give interest and colour throughout the year. To get this effect I would include shrubs, bulbs, coloured foliage and any kind of plant that would ensure a pleasant furnishing at any time of the year.

With such excellent shade plants as geraniums it is not always easy to decide which are the purely woodland types and which are suitable for the more formal planting in a border. I have always kept all the varieties of *G. pratense* in my ditch garden, probably because in my mind they belong to the hedgerows, and though the silver, pink and double forms are exceedingly attractive it is to the wild that they belong. But after seeing the double purple meadow geranium, *G. p. plenum violaceum**, in the violet garden at Sissinghurst Castle I feel I have not given my plants the position they deserve and I have now planted the double white and double blue as well as the double purple forms in shady parts of my terrace garden. I have always had *G. endressii* there, both the type and salmon-pink *G. e.* 'Wargrave'*. There is another more dwarf form which flowers more continuously than either, and I have a deeper-flowered one given to me by Lady Moore of Dublin. All the history she could give me was that it came to her from a clergyman with a black beard, and I'd always give it parlour treatment for that reason. *G. e.* 'Rose Clair' I consider more a woodland plant for although the individual flowers (which are white and veined with crimson) are very pretty they are rather small and the general effect is leafy.

For the same reason *G. reflexum*, *G. punctatum* and *G. phaeum* have to stay in the wild and I think that *G. sylvaticum*, both white and blue, would not show up well in a border although they are lovely peeping from a leafy bank, perhaps because one was not expecting anything but greenery and the flowers come as a pleasant surprise.

G. anemonifolium* comes from Madeira and is not quite dependable so it can be planted in a place where its demise would not be noticed, should such an unfortunate event occur. It needs to be grown where each plant stands alone, for it looks like a miniature palm with its symmetrical arrangement of divided leaves topped by branching flower stems bearing large deep pink flowers. It makes an excellent pot plant and would be pleasant in a shady courtyard. *G. hirsutum* is hardier but not quite so spectacular. I grow it in a shady corner with primroses, hellebores and euphorbias and it flowers when the other plants have green only to offer.

After seeing G. *nodosum* flitting about the wide borders of St Nicholas in Yorkshire I think it would fit in anywhere that is shady and not too dry. It has rather pale leaves which look as though they had been varnished, and the soft lilac-pink flowers appear in an endless procession all through the season.

I am always grateful to G. *atlanticum**that it produces its forest of young growth in the autumn when any foliage is valuable. It does not matter that the leaves disappear after the plant has produced its lovely flowers of blue veined with crimson, for a gap in the summer border is not noticeable then and it is not the time when one starts planting in all the bare patches in the garden.

Evergreen grey-green leaves are an acquisition anywhere, so G. *renardii*, a dwarf with dull-surfaced crinkled leaves, looks well against plants with red or very dark leaves, and its purple-veined white flowers add to the picture. The Chatham Island G. *traversii* 'Russell Pritchard'* should be planted where it can hang down, on a bank or a low wall. The leaves are silvery, with a satin finish and though I suppose one should call the flowers magenta it is that colour at its most pleasant. They keep coming from June to October, in sun or shade, and show up well against their own silver foliage and that of other plants.

Though G. *ibericum** is lovely when in flower its season is short and the foliage is rather untidy afterwards so it is best in any wild shady places. G. *alpinum** is also lovely when in flower but its foliage disappears after turning to straw and it has a wandering disposition, so it has to open its lovely blue flowers in the wilderness, but G. *psilostemon* (G. *armenum*)* has lovely leaves, which turn crimson in autumn after the black-eyed magenta-crimson flowers are over.

I gave G. *delavayi* rather a back seat in a shady corner until I saw how impressive it was in a border in the Savill Gardens at Windsor. Standing alone one could admire the beautifully marked leaves and study the exquisite workmanship of the flowers with their reflexed crimson-black petals, green markings and pointed ruby-red styles. Now I have given it a more worthy position such as is deserved by G. *wallichianum* 'Buxton's Blue', with its trails of mottled leaves and lovely white-centred blue flowers late in the year. The leaves turn red in autumn. G. *grevilleanum* has pink flowers instead of blue, veined with crimson.

The ordinary G. *sanguineum* blooms for a very long time but it is too possessive for many parts of the garden, though the white form, and the pink G. *s.* 'Glen Luce' are not so thrusting. The pale pink G. *s. lancastriense** is a neat and well-behaved version acceptable anywhere. The scented leaves of G. *macrorrhizum* make excellent ground cover and colour well but they need poor soil to keep them dwarf. The deep rose form grows well under the ilex in the National Trust garden at Tintinhull in Somerset. There are forms with soft pink flowers or with white flowers made lovelier by red stems and calyces.

The tall, pale yellow scabious, *Cephalaria tatarica**, which makes up in quantity what it lacks in the size of its flowers, is often grown in sun but it does very well in shade, and so does *Penstemon barbatus* (*Chelone barbata*) with tapering 3-ft spikes of coral flowers. They are slightly reminiscent of miniature foxgloves and need as a background a heavier plant. *Cynoglossum nervosum* has bright blue flowers and grey-green leaves and is a solid plant useful to grow with the penstemon.

*Dracocephalum prattii** also has blue flowers and rather hairy leaves. It grows to 3 ft and looks (and smells) rather like a large catmint. It has running roots and where space is important I plant it in a big drainpipe sunk in the ground. It does not mind a little shade, nor does the running *Nepeta* 'Souvenir d'André Chaudron' ('Blue Beauty')* and the rather spiky *N. nervosa*, with soft blue fuzzy heads.

We are all much indebted to Mr Howard Crane for clearing up the mystery of *Rhazya orientalis** and *Amsonia salicifolia**. These two plants are so alike that only botanists can really tell them apart, in fact there has been a feeling that they are the same, but there are two schools of thought as to what they should be called. For years Mr Crane has been asking me 'How is your *Rhazya orientalis**?' and I always reply that my *Amsonia salicifolia** is doing very well, thank you. Now he has taken the trouble to sort out the mystery and in a letter to *Gardeners' Chronicle* of June 13, 1963, explains that there are, in fact, two distinct plants. *R. orientalis** is a native of Greece, was introduced here in 1889 and takes its name from an Arabian physician of the tenth century.

*Amsonia salicifolia** is a N. American plant and is named after Dr Charles Amson. It is taller and a little less sturdy than rhazya, growing to about 2 ½ ft. Its heads of starry, slaty blue flowers are a little bigger than those of rhazya and flower for not as long a period.

Though I grow both plants it is amsonia that has the first place in my affection. It grows very happily in light shade and soon makes a big colony, for it has roots that wander but do not run. They are shaggy with roots, and send up shoots at intervals. Pieces are easily detached and each soon makes a new plant. The soft colour of the flowers goes well with nearly all shades in the garden, so it is a very good mixer.

Lindelofia longiflora is a member of the borage family and rather sombre with dark green leaves and deep purple-blue flowers. Compared with it, the branching spikes of *Salvia haematodes*, thickly clustered with delicate blue flowers, is gay and carefree. But either of these plants would make a good foil for the rich colouring of *Echinacea*, 'The King', with flowers that are a handsome mixture of crimson-purple and red-brown, with grey undertones against a background of dark leaves.

Soil is more important to it than sun and it will succeed in shade if the soil is rich and fairly moist.

There are many herbs that will grow well in the shade such as Sweet Cicely, *Myrrhis odorata*, which seeds itself profusely if it decides to adopt the garden. Lovage, too, will grow well and fennel I grow as much for its beautiful blue-grey foliage as for its culinary uses, but I cannot go into details of all the herbs that will grow in the shade as there are so many of them.

~ 3 ~

A Shady Border
Late Summer and Autumn

When one thinks of a shady border almost the first flowers that come to mind are the tall anemones, called collectively Japanese anemones (*A. japonica**) which are, in fact, hybrids developed from *A. hupehensis* from China and Japan. Flowering in autumn they provide colour for many weeks and are excellent as cut flowers.

The most beautiful of all, I think, is the pure white single form, just *A. hupehensis alba*, or *A. h.* 'Honorine Jobert' if a named variety is preferred. *A. h.* 'Louise Uhink' is a wonderful plant, tall, stately and large-flowered in pure white, with an extra row of petals which puts it into the semi-double class. *A. alba dura* is also white but the flowers are flushed with pink on the outside.

There are many pinks and if one is lucky to get hold of a good form of the native *A. hupehensis*, there is nothing prettier. It is fairly dwarf, with dark green leaves and flowers that are pale pink within and flushed with a deeper purple-pink on the outside. All these anemones run but I think this is the worst offender, although it is very lovely running at will through a border that is not too formal. It is allowed to do this in the wide borders in St Nicholas, the famous garden created by the late Hon Robert James in Richmond, Yorks. Here the delicate *Geranium nodosum* is doing the same thing and the two together make a picture that I shall never forget.

The deepest pink is *A.* 'Prince Henry', sometimes listed as *A.* 'Profusion'. *A.* 'Bressingham Glow' is also deep pink. Among the paler pinks *A. h. elegans** and 'Queen Charlotte' are good varieties, and *A. vitifolia robustissima** has silvery pink flowers. For those who like double flowers *A.* 'Margarete' is very double with narrow petals arranged like a ruff. *A. vitifolia* is nearly as vigorous as *A. hupehensis* and enjoys itself in a wide border where it can wander about a little. It is a useful plant for shrub borders and blends well with fuchsias and old roses. Though these anemones are so busy when they get into a garden they are like many plants with running roots and do not take kindly to being moved. Some nurseries find it best to grow them in pots and send them out as small plants.

The tall anemones need dwarf plants as associates and the long flowering *Viola cornuta* is a good choice either in white, purple or mauve. It likes a cool, shady position and soon increases to a wide mat. *V. gracilis* is dwarfer and neater in habit, and also flowers for a long time. *V. g.* 'Black Knight' has flowers that are as near black as a flower can go, there are white and yellow forms and some in shades of purple and violet. *V.* 'Martin' in bright purple and *V.* 'Norah Leigh' in lavender-blue are almost always in bloom and so is a little pinky mauve viola named 'Haslemere' and grown by the late Nellie Britton, the well-known plantswoman. I do not find the pale yellow *V.* 'Moonlight' as robust as the others, and I also have difficulty in keeping going that quaint little viola 'Irish Molly', sometimes called 'dirty-faced Molly' because of its strangely fascinating smutty green countenance.

There are lovely shades of pink in sidalceas (Greek mallows) and they have an elegance not found in all herbaceous plants. From neat rosettes of rounded leaves rise 3-ft spikes with flat, satiny flowers. My favourite is still the old-fashioned 'Reverend Page Roberts' with pale silvery pink flowers. 'Crimson Beauty' in deep rosy crimson and 'Sussex Beauty', a medium pink, are among the many good varieties which range from white to crimson and grow happily in shade that is not too dense.

There are certain garden plants that we have hitherto rather taken for granted but which have suddenly become very popular, probably because our gardening ways are changing and we are realising the good qualities of hitherto neglected plants. I would put the day lilies, hemerocallis, in this category. Though we are still a long way behind the Americans in this respect day lilies are getting far more attention than they did a few years ago, and new and more exciting varieties are being produced every year. They are perfect plants for a shady garden that is not too dry, they need practically no attention and flower for many summer months.

H. fulva used to be found in every garden and it is still in circulation. Some shades of orange are very strident but the buff-orange of this flower is quiet and easy to live with. There is a semi-double form made richer by crimson tints, and in both cases the foliage is very sturdy. I have known this day lily all my life and though I am quite pleased to find a shady corner for it I should not miss it very much if it walked out one day, but I would mind if the pale yellow *H. citrina* disappeared. This is rather a small one on slender stems, delicately scented. It tends to take a back seat among the more modern varieties, but it fits into the smallest border and its foliage, like that of all the day lilies, is very helpful among early spring flowers in the border.

H. 'Hyperion' is one of the newer varieties but it gets a welcome from me which some of the others do not because of its pale, lemon-yellow flowers, which are so freely given and are very fragrant.

So many of the day lilies are orange or have an orange tinge, in fact it is difficult to keep the orange out and even the so-called pink hemerocallis have a tinge of buff. One big grower tried for years to produce reds and pinks that had no shade of orange or buff, but the tawny tinge would not be repressed and in the end he scrapped all his day lilies and decided to try no more, sacrificing many acres of plants and years of work.

I hope it will soon be possible to buy the American mauve and purple day lilies in England. Some have quite small flowers and I understand their varieties flower over a longer period even than ours do so that one can enjoy these flowers for many weeks. Some of their pale yellow varieties have a touch of green, which is always fascinating, and *H.* 'Greengold' is now available in England. And so are several pinks, such as 'Pink Charm' and 'Pink Lady', but they are not without their touch of buff. In the coral-coloured *H.* 'Tasmania' there is an overtinge of purple.

Day lilies planted with shrubs would make a very labour-saving border and I know one quite self-supporting shady border where spring bulbs are planted between ferns and day lilies. It is only when the lilies show signs of congestion with smaller flowers that they need dividing.

Most gardening books recommend that peonies should be planted in full sun, but I know many gardens where they grow well in shade and that is the way I like to grow mine. I have one complaint about peonies and that is their very short season, but they do last a little longer if grown in shade. This applies particularly to the species and to tree peonies. I think most people grow the tall yellow *Paeonia ludlowii** as a shrub; it has yellow flowers in May and June and makes a bush as large as 9 ft wide by 12 ft high and its large well-shaped leaves are beautiful for many months. The leaves of *P. delavayi* are also good and its flowers can be, but it is necessary to pick a good specimen. At their best they are glossy maroon with golden stamens, but they can be small and rather a dingy bronze-orange. Usually one grows both these as leafy shrubs for they make wonderful garden furnishings.

The early cream *P. mlokosewitschii*, commonly known as Molly the Witch, is a lovely plant which I have grown for years under the shade of a laburnum, and under a large phlomis in another part of the garden. The flowers do not last long but it has beautiful foliage which turns magnificent shades of crimson in autumn. The flowers are real globes of gold with deeper golden anthers, and their short season is compensated by the brilliant colour when the seed pods open later on. These pods are lined with bright cerise as a background for the black seeds. There are usually a few infertile seeds the same bright cerise, and the whole effect is most colourful.

P. cambessedesii has the same bright pink seed pods. This peony is smaller than the Witch, and has beautiful leaves which are green above and purple below. The flowers are deep rose pink with red filaments. This is not the easiest of peonies to please, I think it is not a long-lived plant anyway, but I find that it does best in the shade and shelter of a low wall and in a well-drained site.

The herbaceous peonies do well in sun or shade, and the old May-flowering cottage peonies, *P. officinalis*, do very well in a shady spot and have flowers that last longer than some of the modern hybrids. One can have them in white, pink and deep crimson and they are just the plants for an informal garden.

I am very fond of the species *P. peregrina*, with its large single flowers of intense scarlet, but scarlet without a trace of orange. *P. p.* 'Sunshine'* is a named variety and there is also 'Fire King' and 'Sunbeam'. I grow this peony in a very shady place and it flowers well. I always admire the way it flowers under the ilex in the National Trust garden, Tintinhull, in Somerset.

Another species peony not often grown is *P. tenuifolia*, with its filigree foliage and single or double red flowers. I grow the single form under a leycesteria and find it flowers well and is the only peony I know that spreads by underground stems. When I first started gardening, in my ignorance I planted this ferny-leaved peony in full sun high on a south-facing bank against a wall. It flowered well but the flowers were fleeting and the plant needed a great deal of water. When I moved it to a well-nourished position under the shrub it was far happier.

The pure white *P. obovata alba**, which has a crimson centre encircled by golden stamens, needs a sheltered position such as is found among shrubs or in woodland gardens. I also grow two other peonies in shady corners, *P. russii** and *P. mascula* (*corallina*), the peony that grows wild on the island of Steep Holme, and which has deep pink single flowers.

It is interesting to note that William Robinson in his *English Garden* is most insistent that peonies should be grown in shade and recommends them to brighten wild gardens. He even gives an illustration of peonies being grown in long grass.

No plants are better for growing in shade than the monk's hoods. Most of the garden varieties flower in late summer but our native *Aconitum anglicum** flowers in April and May and is well worth growing. I do not know how I came to grow it for I do not believe any nursery stocks it but I like it better than some of the cultivated forms (*A. napellus bicolor**, for instance) for its dark blue helmeted flowers are just as good as the garden varieties. Its leaves may not be quite so finely cut but it makes a fine upstanding plant at a time when there are not many blue flowers.

Aconitum 'Sparks var.' which flowers in July has dark blue flowers on branching stems and is an easier plant to group than the solid spikes of *A.* 'Bressingham Spire', which needs to be grown in a position by itself. The two autumn monk's hoods are both beautiful, *A. fischeri** is rather stocky with bright blue flowers and *A. wilsonii** has 18-in spires of rich blue, 'Barker's var.' being the best one to grow.

Few people seem to have discovered *A. napellus carneum**, sometimes called *A. roseum*, but really far more fleshy than rosy. It is rather dwarf but a pleasant neutral little plant for growing with other things. The pale yellow *A. lycoctonum* has far more character but is more difficult to place. Its flowers are rather thin and hatchet-faced and perch on long and rangy stems. They come out in all directions and need staking if they are to make any show. A better way is to grow the plant among shrubs so that its angular flower spikes can grow through their branches.

Much more, I think, could be made of monardas, the homely bergamots of the cottage garden. There is something very voluptuous and satisfying about a well grown *Monarda didyma*, the old-fashioned red form from which the named varieties are derived. I can see little difference between the species and the popular 'Cambridge Scarlet', but the species seems to have rather smaller flowers and the green leaves near the flowers are somewhat stained with crimson. 'Croftway Pink' and 'Mauve Queen' are two other old favourites which remain while newer varieties come and go. 'Adam' and 'Melissa', 'Mahogany' and 'Blue Stocking' have their hours of triumph and then seem to take a back seat. I have had 'Mrs Perry' in deep pink, 'Prairie Glow' in salmon, a pale blue species and one with buff flowers but I have not them now. One new one will, I think, remain with us. *M.* 'Snow Maiden' is a splendid plant, which makes a fine bushy clump and goes on flowering for several weeks.

The roots of monarda are as near to the surface as the bones of a skate and not unlike them. So the plants need a fairly moist position in shade, and if there is time it is a good idea to top-dress the clumps with soil or peat before the winter to bring them safely through.

Moisture is necessary for herbaceous lobelias and though it is usually recommended that they should be planted in full sun the best ones in my garden are those growing in the shade of tall shrubs. They need extra moisture if they are to grow in sun but will do quite well in an ordinary bed if planted in shade but of course should never be planted in a very dry spot. *Lobelia fulgens* is undoubtedly the most popular one to grow and there never seems to be enough of it to supply all demands. It is undoubtedly a very showy plant, almost too colourful when grown in blazing sun but rich and sumptuous in shade. I much prefer the green-leaved lobelia, the true *L. cardinalis*, but for some reason it does not grow as well for me as the purple-leaved lobelias, of which one called 'The Bishop', with rather smoky leaves is the stronger. I have a form with magenta-crimson flowers which delights in the name of 'Kingsbridge'. I have had it for years, it doesn't increase although I have put it in the dampest spot in the garden at the bottom of a north wall. I notice that it has now put itself in a chink at the bottom of the wall, which shows it means to stay.

I find the blue *Lobelia syphilitica* very reliable, particularly in a north border, but I have not succeeded in keeping the one called *L. s. nana* dwarf. I have only to plant it in a shady niche in the rock garden for it to shoot up to 2 ft, and I wonder if there really are two forms of *L. syphilitica*. *L. milleri* is another new variety, which seems very reliable. The white lobelia, which I think is a form of *L. syphilitica* is quite hardy but not very exciting as the flowers are rather small in proportion to the rest of the plant. The easiest of all the lobelias is *L. vedrariensis**, with violet flowers. Some nurseries suggest it is the same as 'Purple Emperor' but I had them both once and they were not the same, *L. vedrariensis** being a much more robust plant with darker leaves and taller stems. It has stayed with me but the Emperor has not. There is also a form with mauve flowers, probably a form of *L. vedrariensis**, which is very robust and increases well.

A dry summer can reduce the ranks of one's lobelias considerably. I once had so many of the pink *L.* 'Russian Queen' that I did not know where to plant them. Now I am reduced to one plant and have transferred this to the nursery, I am so afraid of losing it. This plant has a white spot on each flower and the garden experts who delight in finding a virus in every plant insist that the Queen's beauty spot is caused by a virus. There is another pink lobelia, 'Joyce', with no white spot, but a stronger, bigger plant thereby missing a little of the regal charm. In old catalogues another pink, 'Mrs Humbert', is listed but I have never seen it.

It is a pity that *L. tupa* is not quite hardy. It is a fascinating plant with very pale grey-green leaves, which are hairy and much larger than the leaves of the other lobelias. It has brick-red flowers and is a most handsome plant if one could find a position sheltered enough to keep it. It does well by the sea although not many people seem to know about it.

We usually grow phlox in sun because phlox is an accepted border plant but phlox is really happier in shade. With very shallow roots and flowers that are often very bright this plant can easily be spoilt by too much sun. The ordinary herbaceous phlox are useful plants to grow among shrubs for there their excellent long-flowering habit is particularly useful.

There are a tremendous number of border phlox, all beautiful and in every colour of the rainbow except yellow. In addition to all these beautiful hybrids I think the original *Phlox paniculata*, from which the others have been produced, should be in every garden. It has large trusses of rather small lavender flowers which are very lovely and go with everything else in the garden and last for a long time. The cut flowers might easily be taken for plumbago. The white form is just as lovely and has a grace which most of the border phloxes miss.

There are several dwarf phloxes that are useful for the front of the border, but they also need shade. *P.* x *arendsii* has soft lavender flowers and grows to about a foot. In *P. divaricarta laphamii** the flowers are soft blue and are produced early in the year. It grows from 9 in to 1 ft and must never be allowed to dry out. *P. stolonifera* is 6 in only and has pink flowers. *P.* 'Blue Ridge' is a beautiful plant for shade and good soil, with soft lavender-blue flowers. It never stays long with me and I think is a lime hater like *P. adsurgens*, with its trailing ways and delightful flowers in salmon-pink. I can keep this in a shady lime-free bed but always failed when I grew it in ordinary soil.

Most of the artemisias come in the category of silver foliage and some need a place in the sun but the tall and handsome *A. lactiflora* which likes shade is a most handsome plant with frothing milky plumes over slightly aromatic foliage. It makes an imposing clump in the border up to 5 ft high. The cottage garden artemisia, *A. abrotanum* (Lad's Love or Southernwood) is very happy in shade.

As a general ruling I would say that most of the veronicas do best in sun but there are several that will grow under trees. I have the tall and pale *V. exaltata* growing well under a judas tree, its flowers are a very delicate Wedgwood blue and often grow on 5-ft stems. *V. virginica** is another veronica for shade, with leaves growing in whorls up the stalk and flowers a little darker than *V. exaltata*; there is also a white form of this. *V. michauxii* is a little more congested in its growth with blue flowers. *V. gentianoides* is one of the most useful plants in the garden, doing well in shade and making solid carpets of shining dark green leaves. It is excellent for growing under trees and shrubs and the variegated form is even more attractive with cream splashes on the leaves and sometimes a splash of pink. The tall spikes of very pale blue flowers show up well in dark corners. There is a form with rather smaller flowers on shorter stems and flowers of deeper blue. It is a mistake to leave this veronica without splitting it up regularly. Each rosette replanted separately becomes a bigger, stronger plant.

While most of the achilleas do best in sun the obliging white-flowered achilleas grow well in shade. I say obliging and sometimes they are somewhat too obliging with their thrusting white roots and habit of popping up in the most unexpected places. I can never see much difference between *A. ptarmica* 'The Pearl' and *A. sibirica* 'Perry's White'*. Both have relays of white button flowers over a long period, and 'Perry's White' is said to be a little earlier to flower. They make a most useful cut flower lasting well in water and are good for dried flower arrangements because they remain remarkably white. I now plant them in large drainpipes sunk in the ground. I do not think they stay controlled even with these precautions but they do not get into quite so much mischief.

After the marathon roots of *A. ptarmica* it is a relief to grow the other white achilla, *A.* "W. B. Child'*. No wandering roots this time but rather tight clumps of ferny foliage and small white single daisies, with large centres and short petals. It has not the erect habit of *A. ptarmica*, which stands up to face the world, however much of a nuisance it is making of itself. 'W. B. Child', on the other hand seldom stands up straight and one finds it grovelling about among the ground-cover plants.

I know of one herbaceous phlomis only, which was *P. samia* when I acquired it but now seems to be called *P. russeliana* (*viscosa*; sometimes erroneously called *P. samia*). It grows well under trees and is a comfortable plant for all-the-year beauty. The leaves are like those of the shrubby Jerusalem Sage but bigger. They are hoary and wrinkled and those at the base large and heart shaped. The flowers are valuable because they are pale primrose, so useful in the garden and so difficult to find. It is always interesting to observe the details of phlomis flowers, those generous cushions of labiate blossoms speared by the stem that produces another flower about an inch higher up.

Solidagos are sun lovers as their name would imply but there is one that grows happily under trees. *S. caesia* is an old plant and seldom seen these days but it is worth growing for its good temper and now that gardeners want form and texture as much as colour it holds its own. The long whippy stems look almost black but actually they are purplish and have bloom-like grapes. For the top 6 in and more they are encrusted with tiny dark yellow flowers which mix well with other flowers and last for a long time. And it does not run! Nor does the tall and leafy *S.* 'Golden Wings', which is willing to spread its wide arms in light shade. I grow the greeny yellow *S.* 'Lemore'* in shade, and the other dwarf and well-behaved modern golden rods do not insist on sun. Even *Solidaster luteus**, which used to be called *Aster hybridus luteus* and is a cross between a golden rod and a Michaelmas daisy, will take a little shade and that obliging and cheerful daisy, *Rudbeckia speciosa** (*newmannii*), with its prominent black centres, flowers just as long under trees as in full sun.

Physostegia is one of the most useful autumn flowers for the border. Its popular name of Obedient Plant refers to the flowers and not to the plant itself, which has upright sturdy stems which need no staking and are a comfort when Michaelmas daisies and gladioli are needing all the supports we can give them. Physostegia increases by underground roots but it is never a nuisance and does very well in shade. The old plant *P.* 'Vivid' is still the best I know, and there is a white form which looks very well under shrubs. The new varieties grow too tall, I think, *P.* 'Rose Bouquet' is a lighter shade with branching stems, but it reaches 2 ft and more. *P.* 'Summer Spire' is even taller, its old name of *P. rubra* has not much to do with its colour which is the same orchid pink. There is a new white physostegia called 'Summer Snow' which is an improvement on the old white form, being tightly packed with larger flowers.

Astrantias are useful plants, flowering from summer until early autumn. *A. major* comes from the Continent of Europe, where it grows in alpine meadows and on the edges of woods in Austria and Switzerland. I can hear a gasp of horror when I mention polygonums, but there are several that are well worth growing and do not run too badly. Most of them do as well in shade as in sun, and there are varieties that fit any part of the garden. The improved form of our native bistort, *P. bistorta superbum**, is very pretty growing among other flowers and I put it in a shady border instead of the pink poterium which is far too possessive for decent society. The polygonum has fine deep pink bottle-brush flowers which last a long time. The bright crimson *P. amplexicaule** makes a wonderful mass of colour late in the year, it grows into a big leafy clump and flowers from June until the frosts of autumn. It increases but not very quickly and is a great standby in a big border, its many erect spikes intermingling with the plants around. There is a good white form. The smaller *P. affine** and *P. vacciniifolium** make good ground cover in shade and both flower in autumn. *P. tenuicaule** is another small variety which hugs the ground, has white flowers and does best in shade.

A white polygonum that flowers in summer, never gets very high and has fine white flowers in arching sprays is *P. divericatum*. It has rather a sideways form of growth and does well near the front of the border or under shrubs. *P. paniculatum** is a taller plant, reaching about 2 ft in my soil. I grow mine in a woodland site under apple trees but it would be a good plant for a shady border. There are two polygonums which look shrubby but are really herbaceous that are useful in the autumn. Both are attractive but only one is well behaved. If I had a very large, very wild garden I should let *P. reynoutria** loose in it and be grateful for its jutting sprays of pale pink flowers and know there would be no worry about autumn flowers. *P. campanulatum** does spread but in a more restrained way and it does it in a more visible way with handsome inch-long leaves on the surface, instead of burrowing stems.

Once *P. cuspidatum** gets into a garden it is there for ever. It comes into mine under a wall. I never let it do more than lift up its head but nothing discourages it and it continues to visit. If there was room for it it is really attractive, with handsome leaves and white flowers but it needs to be grown with caution, for dramatic and interesting as it is it is not a plant for the small garden unless the gardener is a fanatic. There is a form at Kew, *P. c. compactum**, which has the most wonderful pink seeds which literally festoon the plant, and of course the red-brown stems of the knotwood are good value in winter.

While most of the large-flowered Michaelmas daisies prefer sun there are several old ones which will do just as well in shade. They are all the small-flowered varieties, *Aster diffusus horizontalis** with its crimson-centred lavender flowers growing on horizontal stems, and some of the *cricoides* (*ericoides*) asters, with tiny flowers and little heath-like leaves. They range from dwarfs of a foot to some about 2 ft high. It is a pity that few people bother about these little asters nowadays. They are delightful with other flowers and pretty growing among shrubs. There used to be one called 'Blue Star', another was 'Mrs G. N. Launder', and it is still possible to buy 'Delight' and 'White Heather', both white flowered, and the 'Hon Vicary Gibbs' in pale rosy lilac. 'Golden Spray' has graceful sprays of small golden flowers.

The *cordifolius* asters will grow in shade too and are fascinating with their heart-shaped leaves and tiny flowers in shades of blue or lavender, many with dark or crimson centres. Old ones such as 'Photograph' and 'Ideal' are still grown in a few gardens, then there is 'Silver Spray', *elegans** and 'Sweet Lavender'. All the *cordifolius* types grow in shade and they stand up in graceful clumps which should not be cluttered up with other plants about the same height.

A. turbinellus 'Lewis Jones' makes a very tall and handsome clump late in the year. The stems are very fine and wiry and are crowned with a cloud of rich blue daisies about the size of farthings. The white *A. tradescantii** is built on the same lines but rather more dwarf and bushier. I am not sure if it is slightly tender or merely choosy about the time it is divided. It has rather a congested woody root and plants divided in late autumn do not always survive the winter, and in the spring they do not recover from the operation very quickly. This aster is still flowering, as a rule, when we have the first frosts, and the fine stems studied with small flowers are quite pretty in the winter when they have turned a warm shade of buff.

The only really big aster that I have found is happy in shade is *A*. 'Empress', with flowers about the size of a sixpence with short lavender rays and large crimson centres. When it first comes out it looks very ordinary and every year I ask myself how ever I allowed such a drab creature to remain in the garden. But after a week or so it becomes a different person, with every stem crowded with flowers so that little foliage is visible. It is then that I thank my guardian angel for keeping me so occupied that I hadn't time to uproot this fine old plant.

~ 4 ~
Shrubs

There should be no difficulty in finding plenty of shrubs to grow in the shady garden, for in addition to those that insist on shade there are many that will grow in a shady place if one wants them to.

First on the list of shrubs that must be planted in shade I would put witch hazels. I struggled many years to grow *Hamamelis mollis* in an open position, my idea being that as it flowered in the winter this is what it would like but the only part of it that grew well was the parent stock on which it was grafted. It was only when I noted that all the best specimens I knew were growing in shade that I discovered what was wrong. The next one I bought was planted under an old apple tree and it has done very well, flowering from December to February and March, and giving warm autumn colour before the leaves fall. There is sometimes a suggestion that witch hazels are lime haters but I planted mine in my ordinary soil, which has plenty of lime. It is often advised that they should be given plenty of peat or leaf-mould and given a position out of the wind as well as out of the sun. I still think *H. mollis* is the best. It is paler—and therefore to me much prettier—than *H. m. brevipetala**, which has deep golden flowers, and more reliable than the lemon-flowered *H. japonica zuccariniana**. It takes a little time to get used to the red-flowered types but they have a charm. The best is *H.* 'Ruby Glow', which has dusky red flowers and leaves that turn red in the autumn. It is sheer prejudice that witch hazels should be yellow, all the same I haven't bought myself a red one yet.

Hydrangeas, particularly the species, really need a shady site and should be planted out of the wind. This applies particularly to *H. villosa**, and *H. sargentiana**. I was recently shown two groups of *H. villosa** in the famous gardens of Dartington Hall, both were in shade, but while one group (in a sheltered place) were magnificent and obviously content, those in a corner where they caught the wind were miserable.

All hydrangeas will grow in shade but the paler shades of the hortensis types are not so insistent on it. The deeper shades are normally more tender and therefore do best in a sheltered position. The lacecap hydrangeas do very well in shade, and of these my favourite is *H. serrata* 'Grayswood', which is rather slow growing and has flowers that change to pink and crimson as they age, and leaves that become deep crimson. I grow it in the shade of a wall. The small *H. involucrata* is good on a large rock garden. It likes shade and has interesting lace-cap flowers which can be blue or rosy lilac. The double form, *H. i. hortensis** is one of the most beautiful small shrubs.

The shrubs that come from Chile can be taken as shade lovers, being used to the jungle. Embothriums are not all hardy and have a glamour that puts them in a class apart but in actual fact *E. lanceolatum** is quite hardy. I have been accused by relations (needless to say) of gardening above my station when I bought this embothrium, which is considered to be the best of the Chilean Fire Bushes. At its best the flower clusters are so thick that they touch and the whole tree seems to be alight. Anyone who has seen them at Bodnant in N. Wales or at Forde Abbey, near Chard, will know what I mean.

*Tricuspidaria lanceolata** is the *Crinodendron hookerianum* of older gardeners, and it needs a lime-free soil as well as shade. It is evergreen and the crimson flowers that hang thickly from the branches in May look like small red lanterns.

Shade and lime-free soil often go together when it comes to shrubs, as they do with other things. Though many of the magnolias do not insist on a lime-free soil they all benefit by plenty of peat and leaf-mould when they are planted, and the early flowering varieties, such as *M. lennei**, *nigra**, *soulangeana** and *stellata* do best in shade as the early morning sun can damage their blossoms. Cold winds can be damaging too so the shelter of other trees or shrubs is good. The June-flowering magnolias which have hanging flowers do best in shade and should be planted if possible where one can look up at the flowers. *M. sieboldii* dislikes lime, but *M. sinensis** and *M. wilsonii* do not mind it.

Corylopsis pauciflora is a lovely March-flowering shrub with pale primrose flowers, which are cowslip-scented. Its heart-shaped leaves turn a rich golden-yellow in the autumn. It needs neutral soil and shade, and also needs protection from wind and spring frosts.

The American May Flower, *Epigaea repens*, is a low-growing, mat-forming shrub for a moist, lime-free peaty soil and any amount of shade. It has beautiful pink flowers and is the embodiment of spring but neither it nor *E. asiatica* are easy to grow unless they have absolutely the right conditions.

Enkianthus, and gaultheria, fothergilla and vaccinium all like shade and dislike lime, and while some kalmias will put up with a little lime if they have shade the charming little kalmiopsis*, with its dark green foliage and tiny brilliant pink flowers, must have both shade and a lime-free soil. Another dwarf that needs the same treatment is the white-flowered *Ledum groenlandicum*, one of Greenland's contributions to gardeners, and the fascinating *Pieris forrestii**, which has new leaf growth a brighter cerise than any flower, is a shrub for shade and no lime. The flower buds are sometimes pink before they open to white lily-of-the-valley flowers. The best pernettyas I have seen have always been growing in shade in lime-free soil, and those with white berries show up particularly well in such a position. To get plenty of berries it is advisable to plant in groups with at least one gentleman among the ladies.

I should include *Skimmia japonica* in my list of shrubs insisting on shade and lime-free soil were it not for the fact that I have a large plant growing in full sun in my heavy limy clay soil. I agree the leaves sometimes look almost variegated, which shows that all is not well although the shrub is covered with berries of several years' standing. All the pundits are agreed that skimmias should be given shade and lime-free soil, so that is what I recommend, and of course male and female plants must be grown together if one is to get berries. I have my 'husband' the other side of the path and though he covers himself with white flowers, deliciously scented of lily-of-the-valley, he is not half as robust as his wife. *S. foremannii** is the hermaphrodite form.

Japanese maples are ideal shrubs to plant under deciduous trees, they need shelter and a neutral soil, and are lovely in sheltered gardens where their brilliant colours and elegant foliage contrast well with other shades and other shapes.

Cassiopes are plants for the connoisseur. They could never be called easy but if one has the right conditions—a moist peaty lime-free soil in shade—they are ideal for the smaller garden where everything is chosen with care and the inmates get personal attention. It is so easy to forget about the things that are planted in a big garden that is very full of treasures. I can easily try for years to find a plant and when eventually I do run it to earth it is quite easy to forget where it is planted. Or you notice something that doesn't look too happy and decide it would be happier somewhere else and then forget where you have put it. Of course the ideal way is to keep a notebook and put down the position of everything in the garden.

Both rhododendrons and azaleas do best in shade and, of course, need soil that has no lime. Although the large rhododendrons are difficult to accommodate in the average garden there are many dwarf rhododendrons that can be planted in small borders or rock gardens. They have small roots so it is not difficult to dig out pockets and fill them with peaty compost. Some people dust the inside of the planting pocket thickly with flowers of sulphur before putting in the new soil. The Alpenrose, *R. ferrugineum*, does not mind lime. The lovely *R. williamsianum*, with bronze leaves and rose-pink bell flowers is particularly insistent on shade as well as lime-free soil. And so are azaleas, for their vivid flowers fade in sunlight. They are shallow rooting and need a mulch of dead leaves to keep their roots cool.

Gardeners do not always agree about the habits of plants and one can only speak from one's own experience in the gardens one knows. *Amelanchier canadensis*, for instance, grows in light shade in my garden. The Snowy Mespilus is a tree of many parts. In April it is snow-white with flowers, which appear among the coppery leaves. There are crimson berries in July but the birds do not let them remain very long. In autumn the leaves turn orange-scarlet and in the winter the twigs give a purple effect.

There is a shady garden I know where *Stranvaesia davidiana** does very well. In April the foliage is bronzy red, in June come its flowers, rather like hawthorn, and then in the autumn the scarlet fruit vies with the scarlet of the turning leaves. It is a slow-growing spreading bush and excellent for a shady mixed border.

Quite a number of the viburnums grow in shade. *V. foetans** is always at the top of the list of shade-loving viburnums. It has pink flowers which are fragrant, and is not unlike *V. grandiflorum*, which has larger, deeper pink flowers, but is not as easy to grow in all gardens. *V. fragrans** is good in shade, particularly *V.* x *bodnantense* with pink flowers, the lovely hybrid of *V. fragrans** and *V. grandiflorum* raised at the National Trust garden at Bodnant.

I have an ordinary guelder rose, *V. opulus*, because I love its greenish snowballs and the wonderful colours the leaves turn in autumn. If I started another garden I think I should be more dashing and have *V. opulus xanthocarpum**, which has yellow berries and makes a smaller tree. Both *V. burkwoodii** and *V. carlesii* seem quite happy in a shady place. One of the best viburnums for a shaded site is *V. tomentosum plicatum**. It is a sturdy spreading bush, with dark leaves, which turn crimson in autumn, and large creamy white snowballs which sit on the top of the branches like small hydrangea heads. I use *V. davidii* for ground cover because of its dense evergreen leaves and sideways habit of growth. Its flowers don't amount to much but its turquoise berries in October are worth the trouble of planting male and female plants together.

Even more brilliant are the berries of *Symplocos crataegoides** (*paniculata*) but the birds like them, while they leave those of *V. davidii* alone. In the Savill Gardens in Windsor Great Park one finds this tree caged when the berries are ripening.

Some people are put off *Leycesteria formosa* because of the number of seedlings it produces, but there are many who are pleased to have the seedlings or they can be used as good foliage for cutting, with their pleasant shape and lovely blue-green colour. The parent shrub gives pleasure at all times, particularly if grown a little above eye level. I have one at the top of a bank so that all its charms can be enjoyed, the graceful arching stems dripping with white flowers which have rich claret bracts, and its stems which are beautiful all through the winter. They are as smooth and green as bamboos and lovely at a time when stems and bark are important. The tree mallow, *Lavatera olbia*, is a generous if not very long-lived plant. But it usually produces a few seedlings and grows quite quickly. Eventually it reaches about 6 ft and has soft grey-green leaves. Not only does it produce a large rose-pink flower at every leaf-axil but it goes on doing it until early winter. By this time the shrub is usually rather big and flabby and I trim off the ends of the branches that might be broken by wind and in the spring cut it to ground level.

Some of the dogwoods have lovely coloured stems in the winter and they don't mind shade. In *Cornus alba spaethii** the stems are red and the leaves striped with gold. In the case of *C. alba* 'Westonbirt'*, which has green leaves and small pale blue berries, the stems are a particularly bright red in winter.

On the whole I think all daphnes do best in shade because they like a cool soil with plenty of humus and do not like to be too dry. This does not apply to our native *Daphne laureola* which likes the deepest shade but does not mind any soil. It puts its seedlings under trees and in the heaviest clay soils. Though nurserymen use this shrub for grafting I grow it for itself. Its tough evergreen leaves are dark and shining and the small green flowers deliciously scented. The commoner types such as *D. mezereum*, *D.* 'Somerset', and *D.* x *burkwoodii* will do anywhere and are quite happy to be in shade, particularly the white form of *D. mezereum* and the larger, stronger white, *D. m. grandiflora alba*.

The yellowish green leaves of *D. pontica* show up well in a shady corner, where it produces creamy green scented flowers without stint. *D. blagayana* does well if it is left alone to wander about in a shady corner producing its richly scented cream flowers at the end of every long stem. The accepted treatment is to keep putting stones over these stems, with the idea of making them root. It is a temptation to oblige the importunate by severing small pieces when they are rooted but this is not at all a good idea, the plant does not like it and soon shows its resentment. The same thing happens if *D. cneorum* is treated in this way. Greed to possess more plants and constant nipping finished off the first *D. cneorum* I had, and now I firmly refuse to sever any rooted pieces but keep on putting stones instead. The variegated form of *D. cneorum* is very pretty with its gold-edged leaves, but it does not like the 'nipping' treatment either and now I leave it quite alone.

The better form of *D. cneorum* is *D. c. eximia** and I have a friend who is most anxious to give me a plant of this for a shady greensand bed of mine. But so far we have failed to establish it. Every time he leaves his lime-free garden near Birmingham he brings a rooted piece of *D. c. eximia** for me, nicely potted up in the right soil. I tend the gifts very carefully, they linger a while before departing. Now I make the donor plant his gifts himself, and he has even taken the trouble to bring a bag of his own soil, but still the plants die. And nearby a big plant of this daphne smirks as it increases and flowers. This came from the Waterperry Horticultural School and has never faltered since it was transferred from its pot to my shady greensand.

Daphnes do best if you catch them young, so I am now fostering small plants of *D. collina** and *D. tangutica* in choice shady spots. The trouble is that the plants outgrow their early niches and you daren't move them. I have a good plant of *D. retusa** that is now in the way of a path after many years of slowly growing up. The path of course, will have to be moved.

I once had a plant of *D. genkwa* on its own roots, that grew out of the shade and into the sun. I foolishly moved it, instead of planting more shade. *D. arbuscula* has died in childhood many times, after being given everything I thought it needed, and if my present charge survives I shall reconstruct the garden rather than disturb it.

*Neillia longiracemosa** is not often seen yet it is a very easy, very pleasant shrub, not unlike a spiraea, with warm pink flowers in May and June. It grows happily in shade for me, as does the bladder senna, *Colutea arborescens*, with its yellow flowers and papery seed pods, which rustle in the wind and are irresistible to children who love to 'pop' them. It can grow to 12 ft but it is not half as high as that under a big weeping willow in my garden.

Flowering as early as February and March, *Stachyurus praecox* a Japanese shrub, is very happy under trees and is strung with soft yellow flowers and has small foliage rather like that of a rubus. *Fatshedera x lizei** both green and variegated, is magnificent tumbling down a shady bank. Not showy but definitely interesting the little twisted *Corokia cotoneaster* is a shade lover. It has wiry black stems which twirl and twist about, its leaves are very small and are silver-backed, to go with its golden flowers.

The common snowberry *Symphoricarpos albus laevigatus**, is beautiful in berry but it can be a pest with its suckering ways. There are several new ones that can be grown without the threat of this menace. They do extremely well in the most uninviting places under trees and as birds do not care for the berries they look as attractive in the winter garden as they do in flower arrangements in the house. My favourite is *S.* 'Mother o' Pearl', with pink-flushed berries on graceful arching stems. In *S.* 'Magic Berry' the berries are cyclamen-pink, and *S.* 'White Hedge' has large white berries growing close to the rather upright stems, which gives the shrub an entirely different character. *S.* 'Constance Spry' is a very good form of the ordinary snowberry. It is, in fact, a superb form, with arching sprays that may be over 2 ft in length and heavily hung with large white berries, but it suckers as badly as any hedgerow plant.

More and more people are discovering what a good garden investment they have in *Mahonia japonica* (or *Berberis bealei* as it sometimes appears). It is a shrub that is good in every month of the year having very good leaves. They often turn delightful shades of crimson in the autumn and, of course, in mid-winter there are sprays of primrose-coloured flowers, scented like lily-of-the-valley. They are inclined to drop when cut but with a big bush this is not serious as there are always plenty more. It does best in shade in a cool peaty soil and can be kept low and spreading if pruned after flowering. There is a rough thickening of the stem about 4 to 6 in below the place from which the flower sprays emerge and it is here that the cut is made and from which new growth will break.

The aristocratic *M. lomariifolia* is not hardy everywhere but those who can grow it place it in the shade where it makes an upright shrub with erect branches clothed with stiff pinnate leaves, and long straight spikes of deep yellow flowers, which are not scented. It is a wonderful sight when fully out but it needs to be tempered by softer, looser plants around it. The homely *M. aquifolium*, or its improved form *M. a. undulata**, would be informal enough for a companion but is far too friendly. It likes to ramble in all directions and so makes good underplanting for trees.

The dwarf *M. nervosa* has always been scarce and after trying to rear a couple of its wayward children I can understand why. Once it gets over its early troubles and is planted under trees in light soil it will run quite happily, and makes delightful ground cover with copper-coloured glossy leaves and primrose flowers.

Our native spindleberry, *Euonymus europaeus*, grows in hedges and spinneys in shade and that is the way I grow it in the garden, for its delicate autumn colour and brilliant old rose berries are as good as those of any of the cultivated spindles. I grow the cultivated forms too, but in more conspicuous places. *E.* 'Red Cascade' is too good a shape to be jammed in with other plants so I keep the surrounding planting low so that one can enjoy the arching boughs which bear many large rosy red fruits. It needs a pollinator nearby, and for this I use *E. hamiltonianus*, which has soft pink fruits and is also bushy and shapely and has to be planted free of distracting shapes. Two more spindles berry well without assistance and have marvellous autumn colour, just as the others have. *E. planipes* has very big fruits which often hang on after the leaves are gone and with their crimson seed pods open showing the orange seeds they are a wonderful sight. *E. alatus* gets its name from the winged bark of its stems, and it too has brilliant coloured fruits.

Only a very severe winter will kill the olearias. For years I had a big bush of *O. gunniana** in a shady corner and visitors exclaimed at the wonderful white Michaelmas daisies in June, and I never had the heart to put them right. In seaside places I get rather tired of olearias at every turn, nearly always white and seldom the rich purple *O. gunniana*, A. M. var*.

Not only do spiraeas thrive in shade but they also do very well in town gardens. *S. arguta** is well named 'bridal wreath' with its arching sprays of white flowers in April. *S.* 'Anthony Waterer Improved'* is a better form of this attractive shrub, with its flat heads of crimson and young leaves in cream and pink. *S. prunifolia plena** has rounded shiny foliage which turns crimson in October and has clusters of button-like white flowers in May. The small star-like flowers of *S. thunbergii* open in March against a background of pale green foliage, which remains fresh until November, when it turns a pleasant buff colour before disappearing, to reappear again in January.

Deutzias, particularly the dwarf forms flourish in shade that is not too dense. *D. x rosea campanulata** is a good white, *D. x elegantissima* is very graceful with pink flowers, and *D. kalminiflora** has large pink and white flowers in clusters over the whole bush.

Bupleurum fruticosum is often seen by the sea but it is equally happy inland and its blue-green foliage and yellow-green flowers are attractive under trees. Forsythias will grow and flower well in shade if the birds let them and so do such cotoneasters as *Cotoneaster simonsii* and *Cotoneaster bullata*.

I wonder if aucuba had not been planted in dreary Victorian shrubberies we should like it better. In those days unimaginative collections of dull shrubs were made to screen the shameful 'tradesmen's entrance' and aucuba would inevitably be there with rusty privets, mangy laurels and the dullest hebes. I always admire the glistening foliage of both laurel and aucuba, and in the case of the aucuba it can be plain green or spotted. Flower arrangers have discovered that the berries, stripped of leaves, are very unusual whether in their green state or when they have turned brilliant scarlet. They are exceptionally large and glossy but one needs to plant male and female plants together to get them. *Danae racemosa*, the Alexandrian laurel is an excellent evergreen shrub for underplanting, only 3 ft high with foliage good for cutting. *Ruscus*, Butcher's Broom, grows in deep shade and in the hermaphrodite *R. aculeatus* Treseder's variety has many red berries and is good for winter decoration.

Privet can be as dull as aucuba but on the other hand it has pleasant scented flowers and given a proper background can be attractive. *Ligustrum compactum*, *L. delavayanum* and *L. japonicum* are all good varieties to grow and the variegated forms of *L. ovalifolium*, either gold or silver, make sensational contrast grown as specimens, either trained against a wall or as informal bushes.

Hebe cupressoides is a shrub with two good characteristics: it is aromatic and it keeps its blue-grey foliage throughout the year, so is well worth growing. Dwarf conifers can transform a mixed border or a rock garden scheme. They will grow quite well in light shade but they do not like to be overlaid by other plants. By using them one can get differing shapes and textures, and colours that range from blue to bronze.

Heathers and daboecias will grow in shade and they make excellent ground cover among shrubs. Most of them need a lime-free soil but the carneas—and there are many of them—darleyensis and the mediterranea group have no objection to lime. The carneas have the great advantage that they flower in winter and are particularly good for making a close carpet. I know a garden where *E. c.* 'Springwood White' is used to cover banks under trees on the way up to the house. The general effect is wonderful and the individual flowers, which are urn-shaped and have brown anthers, are good for picking.

~ 5 ~

Woodland Gardens

There is a great deal of variation in different people's conception of a woodland garden. To me a woodland garden is a garden made in a woodland setting, with most of the interloping undergrowth cleared away and the better of the woodland plants used where they can be seen without a clutter of ranker subjects. There is no question of it being a garden that will take care of itself. Nature is always waiting to take back any territory that has been stolen from her and it is necessary only to think of the hundreds of bramble and older seedlings that appear in a cultivated garden every year to know what will happen the moment one's back is turned.

Nothing can be more lovely than such a garden made under the trees, with a stream if one is very lucky and enough of the vegetation left to make glades and unexpected entrances that lead to wider openings. It has to be pathed, often by artificial means, but the artificiality must be kept as natural as possible. The obvious thing is to keep a grass path closely cut throughout the year, but it depends on the number of people who use it whether it will stand up to traffic. A shady grass path, particularly in wet weather, soon gets worn out if it is used heavily and continually.

When people talk about wild gardens I wonder how wild they are. A moorland garden may remain 'wild' and yet not get out of hand but under trees, particularly if good soil is added for new plantings, everything soon grows most luxuriantly. I have a friend who cleared her wood of brambles and nettles one autumn and planted such things as primroses, bugles and violets. There was no path, as such, and by the following spring, when she wanted to do more planting, nature had taken back her stolen property and the wood was a jungle again with grass, elders, brambles and nettles choking the thoroughfares and growing all over her carefully planted wildlings. If a path had been kept cut there would have been something to work from and she would at least have known where she had done her planting.

There is no better example to follow than the Savill Gardens in Windsor Great Park. There the stream winds under the trees, it is widened here and there and gives glimpses of the garden stretching away into the distance. There are bridges and shallow waterfalls, and the irises and primulas, lysichitum and other bog plants growing at the edge of the water look absolutely natural. Properly constructed paths have had to be made where grass would soon get worn out but the making is unobtrusively done, just as shallow steps that lead from one level to another are made with split logs, and logs are used to make the raised beds round the trees that grow beside the stream.

It needs real artistry to keep a woodland garden looking natural without being too untidy, and to see that the good plants keep their shape and are not swamped by more rampant neighbours and yet do not look formal. Earth between plants must be weeded, and shrubs that sucker and grow rampantly have to be kept in check. The attractive little plants that are imported to act as ground cover if they are any good at all will try to cover everything, and with the ever-present danger of encroachment by the wild the garden soon becomes a jungle again unless it has regular supervision.

The idea of natural grass is very attractive, but it becomes hay if it is not cut and anything planted in it is swamped. Also it is too much the same height as our specimen plants and one loses their outlines. If anything is planted in the grass it cannot be cut until the end of July but it is quite easy to confine one's grass plantings to a wide circle round each tree or in specially confined areas which can be kept 'rough' until all the leaves have died down, while the rest is cut. I do not suggest that the grass should be cut regularly with a motor mower so that it becomes like a lawn, although that is what often happens, but it does need occasional attention from a mechanical scythe, or some implement of that sort. If it is not possible, or desired, to keep the grass in the woodland reasonably short it can be left, but the path must be cut regularly to give meaning to the garden and also to enable the owners to enjoy it even in damp weather for there is no fun in getting soaked to the knees when it is quite easy to keep the path cut.

Planting always raises the old problem of whether we make beds for the plants, which looks too formal, or plant in the grass. The conception of plants growing in grass is a delightful one but it does not work out except in the case of very tough customers such as *Symphytum peregrinum* or *S. tauricum*, foxgloves or sweet rocket, and other plants which are big enough to be cut round. For special specimen subjects one needs to cut out small beds filled with good soil and keep them weeded and clear.

The only plants that can be planted in grass that is scythed once or twice a season are those that die down after flowering. Some of the lilies will naturalise themselves in grass, the martagons, both red and white, and little yellow *Lilium pyrenaicum*. Camassias look lovely grown in grass for they never know what to do with their limp untidy leaves and in coarse grass these do not show. *Gladiolus byzantinus** is a lovely plant, with iridescent flowers in a shade of magenta-pink that tones with most things, but it is an inveterate seeder and comes up in all the wrong places, regardless of other things. I dig it up by the hundred and try to collect the strays into clumps but I never get them all. It looks lovely in grass and under trees and there it can seed to its heart's content.

Fritillaries usually grow in damp meadows so they can be planted if the position is not too dry. I know a garden where the white *Fritillaria meleagris* is naturalised in grass with white narcissi in quite heavy shade. Under one tree the pale green *F. pyrenaica* has naturalised itself and increases well.

Under trees or at the edge of the paths snowdrops and winter aconites can be naturalised. I find the common *Erythronium dens-canis*, commonly known as dog's tooth violet, and muscari (grape hyacinths) grow very well in such places and *Anemone blanda* and *A. apennina* spread very quickly in such happy conditions. The tall *Endymion hispanicus** (*Scilla hispanica*) makes a wonderful picture under silver birches for me, and there it can seed as much as it likes.

If the garden is in a district where wild orchids grow naturally they will often be found in the grass. I know gardens in Hampshire and Dorset, Kent and Devonshire where native orchids have come into the garden and come up regularly every year. The only one that grows well with me is *O. maculata**, with pale lavender flowers and spotted leaves. It is not the most exciting, by any means, but a single plant given me many years ago from a friend's wood in Dorset has sown itself in different parts of the garden, always under trees. I have bought or been given many others from time to time but they never stay with me.

It is the same with cowslips. They will grow where they fancy and cannot be coerced. I have bought them several times for naturalising but I can keep two kinds only, a bright red form given me by a friend, and a beautiful hose-in-hose cowslip which I got from Miss Wynne of Avoca in Ireland. I am now trying to establish hose-in-hose cowslips in soft shades of apricot and hope they will settle down because they are particularly well scented, although I do not think any of the coloured cowslips are as lovely as those with the natural-coloured flowers.

Colchicums are lovely when in flower and nothing could look fresher and more luxuriant than their large and glistening leaves in spring, but their dying-down process is not pretty and a good place to grow them would be in front of shrubs or in grass that is not cut regularly. *Crocus tomasiniamus* is as pretty as anything in the garden but it is as promiscuous as grape hyacinths so if it could be persuaded to grow and do its seeding in the woodland garden we should love it more.

I would never plant any but the wild primroses in grass, and I am afraid these would not be allowed to grow near any of my named varieties or special ones like the jacks-in-the-green and hose-in-hose types which might intermarry and lose their identity. The double primroses, and other special ones I should grow in special beds made up of good soil. The double ones in particular need good food and I am now growing them in beds under which some decayed farmyard manure has been incorporated. The primroses themselves are planted with peat and sand and more peat is put on top of the beds as a mulch, when weather is very dry. These primroses can be grown under trees that are not so dense that the rain cannot get through to them and they do very well in the shade of tall perennials and shrubs that do not take all the goodness from the soil.

The plants that are likely to be mistaken for weeds can well go in a woodland garden, double buttercups, the double cardamine and the double red campion, *Lychnis dioica fl. pl**. They look well among shrubs but need to be planted in beds and not in the grass. Hellebores in clumps rather than in colonies are beautiful in a woodland setting, especially if they are grown a little apart so that the contours of the clumps are distinct. All these need good soil and must not be allowed to dry out. Soil and moisture are not so important for *Trachystemon orientalis*, a magnificent, coarse-leaved borage with large hairy leaves and small blue flowers and *Brunnera macrophylla*, which seem to be happy anywhere so long as it is shady and no woodland is complete without trilliums; they just ask to be included.

Some of the peony species do well in a garden like this for they need shade that is not too dense. The May-flowering *P. officinalis* in crimson, pink or white make foliage that is rather out of proportion to the number of flowers and are good grown informally among shrubs. *P. peregrina* 'Sunshine', with blood-red satin petals, looks well under trees, and the Steep Holme peony, *P. mascula*, which is deep pink. The two tree peonies *P. lutea ludlowii** and *P. delavayi* make large and handsome shrubs with comparatively small flowers in yellow or maroonish bronze, and their foliage is good, but when the leaves droop and fall they are not attractive and I prefer them in an inconspicuous place in a woodland setting.

In leafy acid soil the Tibetan poppy, *Meconopsis betonicifolia*, is a lovely sight with its piercing blue flowers and hairy leaves. I always think the hairy gold foliage is the best part of *M. regia*, which has ochre-yellow flowers and will grow in soil that has a little lime. *M. simplicifolia* has single violet-purple flowers on foot-high stems. The Welsh poppy, *M. cambrica*, is really one of the prettiest plants in the garden and it knows just where to sow itself to make a charming picture. But it is altogether too prolific for any but a woodland garden and there its graceful flowers in yellow or orange show up well against trees and grass. I grow the double Welsh poppy because it is something rare and it does not seed itself, but it has none of the charm of the single form. *Hylomecon japonicum** is rather reminiscent of a small poppy, growing about 8 in with yellow poppy-like flowers and good foliage. It goes to ground completely after flowering and the place should be well marked with a stick. It needs shade and a moist soil and I am not sure that it likes lime because I have never succeeded in making it very happy.

There is no difficulty in planting under most trees, especially if the ground is well dug and mixed with compost or peat. The evergreen or holm oak, *Quercus ilex*, is sometimes difficult because of its habit of dropping its leaves in late summer.

*Cyclamen neapolitanum** is a very good plant to grow under it as it is usually underground and the flowers have not appeared when the oak leaves fall. Beech trees have a bad reputation and it is only necessary to go into a beechwood to see how few things seem to like the dry soil made by its hungry shallow roots. It is strange that the white helleborine, *Cephalanthera damasonium*, which looks so slight and delicate will grow under beeches as its roots are a long way down. I am advised that *Pyrola rotundfolia*, which has dark shiny leaves and sprays of white flowers, will grow and run about under beeches but I have never seen it. I have also been told that the creeping dogwood, *Cornus canadensis*, which I grow in my peat garden, will grow under beeches. I know it likes a sandy peaty soil and I have seen it making carpets under cork oaks so perhaps it does not dislike lime as much as we think. Cyclamen too, will grow under beeches if started off well, and *Anemone blanda* and *A. apennina* if given good soil when planted. The wild arum, Lords and Ladies, is often found in beechwoods and so it is not surprising that some people find that the Italian plant with its marbled leaves, *Arum italicum marmoratum**, will grow in this position. A plant often found in beechwoods is the stinking iris, *I. foetidissima*, so one could also try the form with pale yellow flowers and the beautiful variegated form. *Geranium macrorrhizum* will sometimes grow, *G. endressii* I am told has been known to succeed and *G. phaeum*, Little Niggers, which has small black flowers in its usual form and also has varieties with white or dove-blue flowers. *G. anemonifolium** may sometimes do, as it likes a dry soil and shelter but with any planting under such trees as beeches it is largely a matter of trial and error and what will do in one garden won't in others, so it is best to experiment with small pieces before buying anything in quantity. I never mind seeing the ground under beeches merely carpeted in silvery moss, with an occasional clump of *Iris foetidissima*. The trunks of these trees are always beautiful, the rich brown leaves hang on till the young growth appears, and the first leaves of the beech are the most beautiful tender green of any.

Elm trees are, I think, more difficult than beeches because their roots go further afield and though hungry they are not hungry enough to starve out all weeds. One often sees wild ivy growing up and under an elm so one could try some of the variegated ivies to make a contrasting underplanting. Conifers are as a rule much easier, and there is a new idea of growing seedlings in pine needles which is an indication of their good growing properties. I grow *Euphorbia cyparissias*, violets, and variegated *Vinca minor* under conifers, *Geranium macrorrhizum* yet again grows well in such a position, and the woolly *Stachys lanata*. *Hypericum calycinum* is another plant to grow under trees with the everlasting peas, *Lathyrus latifolius*, *Lithospermum purpureo-caeruleum** and the cream-flowered *Symphytum grandiflorum*.

Some gardeners find a wild garden useful for all the shrubs and plants for which there is not room or a suitable place in the garden proper, laburnums and berberis, mahonias and hydrangeas, with rhododendrons and flowering cherries in the background. The wild spindle, *Euonymus europaeus*, variegated elders and silver birches all look right growing in the wild. And just as redundant shrubs find a happy retreat there are herbaceous plants which are too good to throw away and yet too robust or too leafy for the ordinary garden. I like doronicum with its evergreen leaves and bright golden flowers in moderation but it makes very big clumps and is not a plant that one wants too many times in a border. There are some good hybrid polemoniums that are suitable for more selective gardening but I should hate to abandon the old *P. coeruleum** altogether so its blue spires are seconded to the wilderness, with pulmonarias, bugles and some of the more rampant geraniums.

*Geranium ibericum**, for instance is lovely when in bloom, but it does not flower for long and its dark green leaves on foot-high stems are often untidy. The best one to grow is *G. platypetalum*, with bigger flowers in a deeper colour. One or two plants of *G. pratense* are welcome among shrubs, but when there are a dozen different and attractive shades that are worth growing the only place for them is the woodland garden. The ordinary form has flowers in many different shades of blue, pale grey (in *G. p.* 'Silver Queen') and several shades of pink. *G. sanguinium* is too possessive for anywhere else yet it has such good qualities in its willingness to flower almost every day in the year and pleasant foliage that becomes crimson in late autumn. *G. punctatum** has pleasantly blotched leaves but its flowers are as small as those of reflexum, which are exquisitely formed but rather lost amid the welter of leafage. There is an *endressii* x *striatum** cross which makes big plants of good dark green leaves and large pink flowers, both attractive but taking up a good deal of space for anywhere but a wild garden, and a newcomer called 'Claridge Druce' with red-veined pink flowers will do well in the deepest shade and has good foliage for ground cover. I grow *G. striatum** in my ditch garden. *G.* 'Rose Claire', the white-flowered hybrid of *G. endressii* grows rather big for normal flower beds, although its small pink-veined flowers are very pretty in themselves. *Mertensia virginica*, the Virginian cowslip, is one of the loveliest of spring plants. There is a bluish bloom on the leaves when they push through the soil and they retain their smooth glaucous look when fully grown and topped by arching sprays of hanging tubular flowers in violet-blue. The trusses of flowers are often so heavy that they need support. *M. echioides* is only 6 in and flowers later. It has silvery grey leaves and intense blue flowers in short spikes, and makes a good carpeting plant.

I know tradescantia is often planted in an ordinary border but it never seems to fit in. With its tangle of leaves, buds and stems, it is always a little untidy although the individual flowers are lovely. It looks at home in a cottage garden or in a woodland setting. Sometimes called Spiderwort, Trinity Flower or Moses-in-the-Bullrushes its flowers may be red or white, pink, purple or any shade of blue. *T.* 'J.

C. Wegulin'* is still one of the best, with its light azure-blue flowers, and the lavender-flushed white of *T.* 'Iris Prichard' is enhanced by violet stamens. The most dramatic is *T.* 'Osprey' which has dead-white flowers each with a raft of brilliant blue stamens.

Lactuca bourgaei is a robust member of the lettuce family with large heads of soft lavender flowers and fresh green leaves. A gigantic cow parsley *Heracleum mantegazzianum*, sometimes called Giant Parsnip or the Cartwheel plant gives a tropical effect, growing as it does to 8 to 10 ft, and sweet rocket, with its scented white or lavender flowers is pleasantly informal and seeds itself mildly.

Honeysuckles should clamber up trees or even festoon small rough bridges if the garden has the added joy of a stream. Species clematis are not out of place in such a setting and if the ground is uneven and it can be contrived to have a path from which to look down on the tops of trees and shrubs such clematis as montana and chrysocoma make attractive canopies. *Clematis flammula* has small white flowers but they are produced generously and are deliciously scented, in *C. f. rubro marginata** they are margined with purple. *C. tangutica* and *C. orientalis** make a lot of growth and their silky seed-heads look particularly well under trees.

Ferns are very much at home in a woodland garden. I like the Hart's Tongue Fern, *Phyllitis scolopendrium**; the fronds are very attractive as they uncurl. The lacy fronds of the Shield Fern, *Polystichum angulare**, are delightful, too, and a good contrast to the solid fronds of the Hart's Tongue. Beside the water, ferns and primulas soon seed and multiply, meadow sweet and lythrum may appear from nowhere, and foxgloves will sow themselves everywhere. In such a garden nothing looks out of place. An ordinary elder may hobnob with a flowering cherry and wild mint will not be snubbed if it comes up as a background for asiatic primulas.

~ 6 ~
Bulbs and Corms

A shady garden is an ideal place for bulbs. Not only do the bulbs like to grow in shade but they are more attractive and look more at home under trees than in the open. We all know how lovely daffodils look naturalised in grass; with trees above and the green background it does not matter how yellow they are. But put a line of 'King Alfred' or 'Rembrandt' in a sunny bed and they become deeper in colour and look almost garish against the soil.

Some of the miniature daffodils that grow in Spain, France and Morocco do best in full sun so that the bulbs can ripen and so produce flowers, but there are many small daffodils that are not collectors' pieces that can well be naturalised. I grow many named varieties in my ditch garden, where they flower quite well, *Narcissus bulbocodium*, the hooped petticoat daffodil, *N. cyclamineus* and its hybrids such as *N. c.* 'February Gold' and *N. c.* 'Peeping Tom'. The Tenby Daffodil, *N. obvallaris*, Queen Anne's daffodil and her jonquil, 'Pencrebar', and the old Queen of Spain all do well for me under trees, and *N. nanus**, *N. canaliculatus*, *N.* x *mini-cycla**, *N.* 'W. P. Milner' in delicate cream, and 'Thalia' in white.

Only hardy cyclamen will grow in the dry soil among shallow tree roots but it is possible to make raised beds in such positions where various bulbs can be grown. Many bulbs do very well in such a position as they are kept comparatively dry by the leaves of the trees. Stones, logs or even old railway sleepers can be used to make the surrounds for the beds, which are filled with a good planting loam. I know one garden where this has been done to house a collection of dog's tooth violets (erythroniums). These hardy lily-like plants vary in height from 2 in to a foot and come in many different colours. They get their name from the tubers, which are pointed and look rather like dog's teeth, although that does not account for the 'violet', which they are not like.

The commonest is *E. dens-canis*, which grows in European woods and has leaves mottled with dark purple and flowers that can be white, pink, lavender or ruby. It is very easy to grow and seeds itself freely when once it has settled down. I grow it in grass under trees and the hanging flowers are very pretty nodding among the green. There are also forms of *E. dens-canis* from the Caucasus, Siberia and Japan in white and cream, pinkish purple and violet.

Some of the better colours have been given names, such as *E. dens-canis* 'Snowflake', which, of course, is white, 'Rose Beauty' and 'Pink Perfection' are soft pink and 'Franz Hals' a light reddish violet.

E. revolutum grows in wet areas from Northern California to British Columbia; it is usually rose-pink with mottled leaves but there is a beautiful cream form called 'White Beauty'*. *E. tuolumnense* also comes from California and has golden yellow flowers and rather large pale green leaves, which are smooth and very handsome. It can stand a dryer position than *E. revolutum*.

There are many beautiful varieties of erythronium, mainly from America, from the creamy white *E. californicum* to the big golden *E. grandiflorum* and many enthusiasts are busy collecting them. Coming from woods and cool meadows they like shade, and the eastern species like a position that is dry in summer.

Snowdrops are ideal bulbs for shade, with one or two exceptions. Those that flower in the autumn, *Galanthus nivalis* subsp. *reginae-olgae**, *G. n. cilicicus** and *G. n. corcyrensis** do best in an open sunny position and I have read that *G. elwesii*, with its rounded flowers and wide glaucous leaves, likes sun, but it grows and flowers very well for me in shade. The rest of them undoubtedly enjoy shade and good drainage.

I do not think the interesting varieties show up very well grown in flat ground under trees. This is a good place for naturalising the more ordinary types such as *G. nivalis*, and nothing is more beautiful than ground under trees carpeted with snowdrops, but collectors' pieces want a position where they can be seen from all sides as clumps. I grow mine between the stones that hold up the banks of the ditch and I hope the supply of such positions will hold out for all the new snowdrops I acquire. I also grow them in the raised beds, like 3-sided troughs, I made against the east wall of the malthouse. Grown thus they stand out with all the beauty of their leaves and arching stems.

Many of the named snowdrops are quite large, almost giants. The largest I have, where the flowers are an inch at least in length, is named after the late John Gray. It was given to me by a collector and I do not believe is available in any other way. Its well-shaped flowers are even bigger than *G. n.* 'S. Arnott', sometimes called the giant snowdrop, which is scented and has 10- to 12-in stalks. *G. plicatus* is very distinct, with its wide 'pleated' leaves and has several variations. This is known as the Crimean snowdrop and according to the late E. A. Bowles many of the snowdrops now growing in this country came straight from the trenches after the Crimean war. I have an interesting snowdrop, given me by a friend, which has double all-green petticoats. Its leaves fold back at the edges and experts think it is a form of *G. plicatus*.

G. elwesii, *G. caucasicus* and *G. elwesii whittallii** are similar, with very glaucous wide leaves and flowers made interesting by the different shapes of the green markings.

The common snowdrop, *G. nivalis*, has some interesting variations, *G. n.* 'Magnet' sways on a long curved pedicel and in *G. n. scharlokii** the spathe is divided. *G. allenii*, with rather yellow-green broad leaves is a big one, growing 9 to 12 in, and in *G. n. viridapicis** the outer segments of the flowers have interesting green markings.

There are several snowdrops with green leaves: *G. ikariae* subsp. *latifolius*, flowering in February to March, and *G. ikariae* subsp. *ikariae*, which is one of the last to flower. There is also a form of *G. plicatus* with green leaves.

Collecting snowdrops is a growing cult. We compare, covet and contrive to get new and exciting ones. There is a fragile little treasure with yellow markings on its petticoat, *G. nivalis lutescens**, found by a Mr Saunders, of Cambridge, in an old Northumberland garden. It survives with me but does not increase and I wonder how it survived so long in that old garden. Another with yellow instead of green markings is *G. n. flavescens** and that has not much stamina either. The double forms of these seem stronger and with me increase well. There is one that was found at Harwood Hall, the Cheshire home of Sir Graeme Elphinstone and named by Samuel Arnott 'Lady Elphinstone'. It is pleasant to have these unusual types but they have not the chaste beauty of the normal snowdrop with its purity. A snowdrop to me is white and green, and when yellow comes into it one thinks of leaves that are turning yellow with age.

G. 'Merlin' goes to the other extreme and his inner segment is practically all green, which seems healthier. In *G.* 'Colesborne' (another which is slow to increase) the green petticoat is edged with white, and one given me as *G. n. virescens** but which has raised doubts in the minds of some experts, is also very heavily marked with green. It is tiny and difficult; in some years the green hands holding up its small white head never let go and the flower does not open.

Collecting snowdrops can be complicated. Some varieties are quite easy to distinguish. *G. graecus*, for instance, can never be mistaken for each of its narrow glaucous leaves is twisted although the markings on the petals vary. There are several types of double nivalis; *G.* 'Straffan', which is single and produces two flowers from each bulb, is slightly different when obtained from different gardens (Mr Bowles' version is most distinct) and there are several forms of *G. plicatus*. Snowdrops seed themselves very liberally and when various varieties are grown close together interesting variations are bound to appear, and, of course, one can do the hybridising one's self. Snowdrops will flower from seed in three years and germination is best, according to Mr Bowles, if the seed is sown directly it is ripe and the whole pod sown directly it is uniformly yellow, without separating the seeds. Mr E. B. Anderson has produced several new varieties; one, which he has called 'Mighty Atom' has a flower very large for its height and there are some strange and fantastic forms more interesting than beautiful and rather reminiscent of some modern art.

Snowflakes (Leucojum) have not the ethereal charm of snowdrops but they too are lovely bulbs for a shady garden, if the soil is moist and rich with humus. *L. vernum* always surprises me when it appears in January and February. It is such a sumptuous flower for mid-winter, with glistening white flowers, pleated and curved to tiny green points, with leaves that are wide, dark and substantial. This snowflake has a faint scent of violets. In the form *L. v. carpathicum** the petals are tipped with yellow, which is not really an improvement. *L. v. wagneri** is characterised by two flowers on each stem.

A shady bank is a good place for the summer snowflake, *L. aestivum*, or a narrow shady border, where the long stems can arch gracefully amongst a forest of tender green leaves. The flowers are very small for the length and thickness of the stems, even in the improved version, *L. aestivum* 'Gravetye'*, but they are exquisitely formed and coloured and have a fascination that grows with long acquaintance. The tiny autumn snowflake *L. autumnale* is a subject for troughs and small rock gardens and will grow in sun or shade. It has small pink-tinged white bells on 3-in stalks and increases quite quickly.

All the anemones are shade lovers and when they are happy they increase very quickly, such species as *A. apennina*, *A. blanda* and *A. nemorosa* certainly do, spreading through shady borders and under trees. *A. apennina* is usually clear blue, and there are white forms and others in darker, richer blue. In the same way there are variations in the colours of *A. blanda*, ranging from white and a light mauve-pink to a deep blue, *A. b. atrocaerulea**. *A. b. scythinica** is white inside and has dark blue backs to its petals.

The ordinary little wood anemone, *A. nemorosa*, is quite attractive enough for the wild garden and its various forms are worth collecting to grow in any shady spot. *A. n. allenii** and *A. n. robinsoniana** have large lavender-blue flowers, there was a lovely double white, and another called *A. n.* 'Vestal', which has a centre of petaloid anthers.

The little yellow anemone, *A. ranunculoides*, has rather small flowers and somehow misses the attractiveness of the others, although the form, *A. r. superba**, with bronze leaves and rather darker flowers, does its best to get into the picture. The snowdrop anemone, *A. sylvestris*, is taller than the others, growing to 15 in, and hangs its white flowers until they open. It has a pleasant scent and needs a leafy soil in its shady corner.

It is easy to get muddled between the scillas and hyacinths. The scillas are a big family and range from 'squills', *S. sibirica**, to the tall *S. hispanica*, now known as *Endymion hispanicus**. The best known of the hyacinths is *H. amethystinus**, like a small bright blue bluebell, and *H. romanus*, sometimes known as *Bellevallia romanus**, which makes a low, compact clump with lavender-blue flowers.

Some of the scillas can be rather too generous with their offspring. One can enjoy the graceful groups of white, blue and pink *S. hispanica** growing among shrubs, but when the blue form, which is the biggest and most robust, establishes itself in the middle of special plants, one's admiration tends to diminish. It would not be serious if it were easy to remove the outsider, but this is not so. They have no intention of being removed, putting themselves down so deeply that to get them out without damaging the other plant is impossible.

The soft blue *S. messeniaca* is almost as determined. It is only 6 in high and lovely as a blue carpet under trees, but when the carpet unrolls in all directions whatever else may be growing, it can be disconcerting. When the flowers are coming out and the clumps are dwarf and neat there is no complaint; it is when they are over and have become lank, yellow and unappetising that one has second thoughts.

My favourite scilla is *S. tubergeniana**, that appears in February, pushing up flowers like big pushkinias in an ethereal shade of Wedgwood blue, made more lovely by stripes of turquoise-blue down each petal. I plant it wherever I have a small shady corner that is dull, for this *S. tubergeniana** never is.

No one can help becoming lyrical about the beauty of grape hyacinths, muscari. The little flowers are perfectly formed in a lovely shade of china-blue, with a white edging, in a texture that is difficult to describe. They are carried on sturdy stalks and make excellent flowers for cutting. But one's enthusiasm dwindles when the numerous seedlings come up in every part of the garden, in the middle of one's choicest plants, tiny cracks in paving and between stones in the rock garden, and other places from which it is difficult to dislodge them. I would not like to be without grape hyacinths but I do not know where it is safe to plant them, and even if they are not seeding themselves all over the place the mass of grassy foliage after the floral display is over is not exactly pleasing. If one has a tall hedge next to a gravel path nothing looks better than a border of grape hyacinths at the bottom of the hedge, and there they cannot get up to much mischief.

The less ordinary types are not nearly so promiscuous or untidy. I have never found a seedling of the tiny white *M. azureum album** or the small Cambridge blue *M. azureum* (*H. azureus*). There is a very dark, almost black, variety, *M. paradoxum**, and a bicolor, *M. latifolium*, pale blue above dark blue, *M. racemosum** in deep navy blue and very dwarf, and *M. neglectum* black-blue. *M. viridis* is a greenish blue and very sweetly scented, as is *M. moschatum flavum**, which starts purple and ends pale yellow. Many people grow the ostrich feather grape hyacinth, *M. comosum monstrosum**, but not so often the tassel hyacinth, *M. comosum*, which is greenish with a purple top. All the grape hyacinths are happy in shade.

Brodiaea, or 'fool's onion' is the Californian hyacinth and most of the genus like a warm spot against a south wall, but the deep blue *B. laxa** will grow very well in shade. I know a garden where there is an extensive planting of this brodiaea under trees, and I am told by the owners that they bloom every year for weeks on end. This brodiaea also grows in the rock garden at Bodnant with gentians and cyananthus. Here it gets shade from the considerable stones and a few trees, and is not completely shaded but certainly not in full sun.

The lovely autumn-flowering colchicums will grow anywhere and are perfectly happy under trees, and flower well. In fact it is a good place to grow them because once planted they need no further attention, and when the large fleshly leaves appear in spring they fit in well if grown under trees and on the borders of shrubberies. The family includes the meadow saffron of our countryside, *C. autumnale* (lavender), *C. a. album**, white and *C. a. minus**, which is 6 in only and rosy purple in colour. There is also a double form of *C. autumnale*, *C. speciosum* var. *bornmuelleri* is large and a deeper colour, and *C. byzantinum* has star-shaped flowers. *C. speciosum rubrum** is most handsome with crimson-purple cups on deep purple stems, and *C. s. album** has great glistening white cups. *C. agrippinum* is a dwarf, chequered in lilac-purple.

There are many named colchicums among the hybrids, 'Violet Queen' and 'Autumn Queen', 'The Giant', 'Lilac Wonder' and 'Disraeli', a light blue. The double colchicum 'Water Lily' is very large and rosy lilac in colour.

There are autumn and winter-flowering varieties among ordinary crocus but they do best in sun, although the autumn-flowering *C. byzantinum* will take a little shade and *C. speciosum* can be naturalised in shrubberies. The spring-flowering crocus are more bulbs for sun than shade, although they can be naturalised in grass under trees and under deciduous shrubs and for this the larger varieties and *C. tomasinianus** types are best. When naturalising crocus it is better to keep the colours in groups. White goes well with either purple or yellow, but if purple and yellow are to be planted in the same lawn they should be in separate groups and not too close together.

Whenever I am asked what will grow under trees I always recommend hardy cyclamen. They seem to delight in the dry shade under trees and sometimes sow themselves between the great gnarled roots of big trees where they can have very little soil. Once planted under trees they will sow themselves all round, and will also grow under pines. They are very happy in beds under hedges, and that is where I grow some of them in my garden. Having no big trees I plant *C. neapolitanum** and *C. n. album**, and *C. repandum* under hedges of *Lonicera nitida*. I like to see the white and pink forms growing separately and as cyclamen take no notice if they are lifted and replanted when in full flower any white ones that appear in the wrong place are immediately planted where they belong, and vice versa. I give them a top-dressing of peat when they are about to flower, more for aesthetic than practical reasons, but they seem to like it. My dream is to have a solid band of cyclamen under every hedge with their butterfly flowers in autumn and handsome marbled leaves for most of the year. Every seedling is rescued and replanted, so far I have left it to nature to sow the seeds, but doubtless there would be many more plants if the seed was collected and sown systematically.

C. repandum will naturalise itself nearly as fast as *C. neapolitanum** and that is planted under hedges as well, but the winter-flowering types, now lumped together as *C. orbiculatum** do not increase so fast for me as the others, and so far I have enough room for them under my small cypress. The corms never get very big as *C. neapolitanum** does. A gardener in a very old garden told me that a corm of *C. neapolitanum album** he once had to lift was as big as the top of a dustbin, and many of mine are 9 or 10 in across. The only cyclamen I do not grow in shade are *C. graecum*, *C. africanum*, *C. europaeum** and *C. pseud-ibericum** which seems to do best wedged under a rock on a high south-facing bank.

Connoisseurs are rather inclined to look down on ornithogalums as being rather ordinary and very invasive but I have never found them a nuisance and they are certainly attractive for naturalising in shady corners. The most ordinary, of course, is *O. umbellatum*, the Star of Bethlehem, with green markings on its white flowers. *O. nutans* is really like nothing else, for I know of no other flower that is really silvery grey, which is what this one is, and combined with pale green it is a most fascinating flower. The two tall ones, *O. arabicum* and *O. pyramidale*, have tall spikes of snowy blossoms and are as good in a shady border as *Galtonia* (*Hyacinthus*) *candicans*, with its large white snowdrop flowers.

Green flowers are always fascinating and the green *G. princeps* is the colour of alabaster. It is not so tall as *G. candicans*, growing only about 12 to 15 in, and doing best in a border that is open but faded from the sun.

Zigadenus is another family which has some varieties that are green, the most attractive—to me at any rate—being *Z. elegans*, which is really pale green and not greenish white. It grows very straight and has rather small green flowers on 12-in stems. I grow it in shade, which it seems to like.

There are several green varieties among the fritillaries. This is a very large family and there are enough easy attractive varieties for most ordinary gardeners. The real collectors have to grow their treasures from seed usually, as corms are not yet available, but seed is usually obtainable. And then comes the long period of waiting. I visit regularly the garden of a very well-known collector and as we look at the rows of pots in the greenhouse containing his fritillaria he always says sadly that he wished fritillaries did not take so long from seed. I have no greenhouse and certainly not enough patience to protect the young plants through years of waiting and I am very pleased to have the varieties easily obtainable.

Our native snake's head fritillary, *Fritillaria meleagris*, the easiest and least expensive, is still one of the most beautiful, especially when growing in grass. When at home it is found in damp meadows in various parts of the country, but when it comes into our gardens it does not insist that the ground shall be damp but it likes shade. I grow it in grass under apple trees and under a sycamore. The little chequered flowers are fascinating and it is difficult to find two alike, but it is the pure white one that melts the hardest heart. It can be bought separately, apart from the mixed varieties, and how lovely it looks in a dark corner under trees.

Some of the best forms of *F. meleagris* have been honoured by being named after the gods, and one goddess—for a very large white is called 'Aphrodite'. 'Poseidon' is also a fine white-veined with purple, 'Artemis' is a soft grey-purple, 'Charon' very dark purple, 'Sulphanus' cream and mauve and 'Saturnus' is chequered in as near a pink as a fritillary will go.

My next favourite is not very rare either for *F. pyrenaica* comes from a wide area and has many variations. The green bells hang demurely and give no indication of the glories within. Inside they are beautifully pencilled and marked with green and brown, and I grow mine in a trough by the garden door so that I can lift their heads and enjoy their hidden beauty several times a day. *F. pontica* is also green with brown lips, and *F. ruthenica* has a greenish mottled lining to its brownish black flowers. *F. bithynica* (*citrina*) and *F. pudica* are small and pale yellow and *F. pallidiflora* is very handsome with large creamy bells. *F. acmopetala* is also greenish yellow with maroon markings. One of the tallest is *F. persica*, which has many small hanging bells the colour, and with the bloom of, ripe grapes. It doesn't look like a fritillary. In *F. verticillata* and *F. v. thunbergii** (*Uvularia cirrhosa*) the cream-coloured flowers are veined with green.

The stately Crown Imperials used to be in every garden when I was a child. Nowadays it is in cottage gardens that one usually sees them, grown in a row, or in old-fashioned gardens. The famous variegated *F. imperialis* still grows under trees in the late E. A. Bowles' garden, Myddelton House, Enfield and there does seem to be a renewed interest in these showy plants, which get their name from the crown of green leaves above the pendulous flowers. They are not cheap to buy, and they can be yellow with pale green, which I think is the loveliest, to various shades of orange and coppery or rusty reds. In heavy soils moisture sometimes settles in the centre of the bulbs and causes decay, and to avoid this the bulbs can be planted with a slight tilt to one side.

In the same way lilies-of-the-valley are being taken more seriously today. In Victorian days when gardens were big, lilies-of-the-valley and ferns were the answer to any shady places that needed filling, and we still find great tracts of these lilies under the north walls of large Victorian kitchen gardens. They are usually overcrowded and haven't been fed for many years but continue to flower profusely with patient forgiveness. One reason why these plants are allowed to get overcrowded is because they resent being disturbed and there is little flower the first year from a new bed. One way that can be used is to take out large lumps here and there in the bed and fill the holes with good soil, using the pieces removed for a new planting. Bonemeal is the best stimulant to give them and they appreciate a mulch of leaf-mould in March.

Lilies-of-the-valley naturally lead us to the other lilies, which are ideal plants for shade, particularly the light shade found among shrubs and under tall trees. It always seems to me that lilies were easier to please in my youth than they are today, and I can remember most lovely lilies in quite ordinary gardens. I do not think they were so prone to disease, one did not hear so much about lime haters and lime lovers, and they were planted without any special treatment in ordinary beds. Nowadays even the gardeners who grow lilies well make special beds for them, very open beds raised by peat blocks so that good drainage is assured, and filled with good soil containing plenty of peat or leaf-mould. The bulbs themselves are always placed on a little bed of sand. Most lilies are given a layer of well-rotted cow manure after the bulbs have been covered with an inch of soil, then more soil is added and lastly a mulch of leaf-mould or bracken to prevent them drying out.

Broadly speaking I think one could say that most lilies prefer a lime-free soil, some, like *L. martagon, L. pyrenaicum,* and *L. regale,* have no objection to lime and *L. henryi* needs the addition of lime in a peaty soil. Lilies seem to grow better in some gardens than others and when a gardener discovers which lilies grow well in his garden he does well to stick to them.

In my heavy clay soil I find *L. regale* the easiest to please and as it is one of the loveliest I have no complaints. It does seem to be better in tubs, large pots or even at the back of large troughs against a shady wall. The Madonna lilies, *L. candidum,* need a position that is open near the ground, so that the young growth is not swamped, but is happy with trees above. I have grown *L. longifolium* in the same way but it does not care for my lime and is not really happy. But both the yellow and red forms of *L. pyrenaicum,* the red and white martagons, and for some strange reason the Bellingham Hybrids put up with me when the tigers, panthers (*L. pardilinum*) and, of course, *L. auratum* and *L. speciosum* are definitely not interested.

As a general rule it is better to plant bulbs and corms from South Africa in sun but schizostylis is, I think, the exception. I used to grow mine in the sun until I discovered how well they flowered under the shade of old apple trees. Moisture is far more important to them than sunshine; drainage is necessary, and I think they should be divided regularly and replanted with some dried blood. I always use sand and peat as well but this would not be necessary in a light soil. They do very well at the edge of a gravel path, in sun or shade, and in a very bad winter it is the Kaffir lilies in the gravel that do best and flower most. There are three forms of *S. coccinea*, the ordinary cherry-red, the large giant form and one found by Professor Barnard and named after him which has more open, starry flowers, and is lighter in colour. It is now possible to buy 'Giant hybrids' and we are all hoping for something unusual to be among them but so far they are large red forms only. I know of two pinks only, the deep shrimp-pink 'Mrs Hegarty' and the paler 'Viscountess Byng' which flowers from October to December. None of us has found a white schizostylis, I feel sure that there must be one in South Africa but it has not got to England yet.

~ 7 ~

Plants for Damp Shade

Happy is the gardener with a stream or a damp corner in his shady garden, for there are many exciting things to grow. Lovely plantings can be made under the trees with paths of flat stones let into the soil, and wonderful effects can be achieved with gunneras and rodgersias, primulas, ferns, iris and many other things.

The majestic gunnera needs plenty of room for one leaf can be 10 ft by 8 ft and a grown plant may take up to 30 ft. *G. manicata* comes from southern Brazil and has great umbrella leaves, bristly and deeply cut, on gigantic stems. These stems are prickly with dark bristles, rather like the works of an old-fashioned musical box, and the coarse root crowns are covered with light brown fur. The flowers are in keeping: nothing feminine and 'pretty' would go with such solidarity, but how effective are the great bottle-brush spikes in green and brown. They turn reddish later in the year and should grow to 3 ft if they get enough moisture in the growing season. The first frost ruins the splendour of this plant and the dead stems and leaves should be piled on top of the crown, with extra leaves, bracken or straw in very cold climates.

Rodgersias with their fingered leaves and fluffy flower spikes in cream or pink also need plenty of room and lose half their attractiveness if crowded in with other plants, but they do not begin to compare in size with gunneras. *R. aesculifolia* is the largest and grows to about 4 ft. Its name gives the clue to the shape of its leaves, which are like those of the horse chestnut, and are crinkled, rich bronze in colour, and grow on hairy stems. The flowers unfurl like an opening fern and grow in heavy spires of pale creamy pink. The leaves of *R. pinnata superba** are copper-green and very deeply wrinkled. They make a fine background for the tiered spires of pink flowers, which later produce reddish brown seeds. *R. tabularis** has round, notched leaves which are pale green and held like umbrellas on thick stalks, with a froth of creamy white flowers above.

The Umbrella Plant used to be called *Saxifraga peltata* but that has now been changed to the cumbersome *Peltiphyllum peltatum**. This is a good plant to grow at the edge of a pond or on a damp slope because the creeping rhizome—which look like the trunks of baby elephants or a complicated wind instrument—will bint the soil together and make a heavy mat. In spring bare red stems rise from this solid mass to open to wide heads of starry pink flowers, and it is only after the flowers are over that the umbrella leaves appear.

Lysichitum*, which is similar to Skunk Cabbage, needs a very damp position, either in a bog or at the edge of a stream, and though often planted in sun will grow very well in shade. It needs room, for the great leaves which follow the flowers last for a long time. In L. americanum* the flowers are yellow, and they come up through the soil in early spring like giant arums with green spadices. The leaves that follow are enormous and their rich green luxuriance makes a strong note among flimsy plants. I think this plant with its strong colours and simple outlines needs nothing but a green background, or, if one must, small white flowers are the only possible mates. Sometimes it is associated with plantings of Primula rosea but that gives too much richness to please me, for both are strong coloured and need the scene to themselves. Actually I prefer the Japanese version of the Skunk Cabbage, L. camtschatcense*, with its pure white flowers with their white spadices and smaller grey-green leaves, with a surface that is more luminous rather than glossy.

The groundsel family has been divided. Some of the senecios are now called ligularias, S. clivorum, for instance, is now L. clivorum*. Again it needs the scene to itself. It has large leathery leaves in dark green, which are heart-shaped, and clusters of vivid orange daisies on very stout stems. In L. c. 'Othello' the leaves and stems are dark purple giving a very rich effect. 'Desdemona' is somewhat smaller, as a lady should be, with rich reddish green leaves lined with crimson, which fade to a metallic green. Most of the other ligularias prefer sun but I grow the Polish L. przewalskii in damp shade. It is a slender plant with tapering spires of tiny yellow flowers and deeply cut foliage.

The senecios, which are still called senecios, also like a damp position. S. tanguticus* is a most handsome plant but we should love it more if it didn't wander so far afield. Plant it at one end of a border and it will come up at the other, but put it in a fairly dry position and it keeps to its proper place. It is a lovely plant and I wouldn't want to be without it, for all its wandering ways. The foliage is very handsome, almost heraldic in its outlines, and the triangular spikes of flowers beautiful at all stages. First come the yellow flowers, which are tempered with green and never too crude. They are followed by fluffy silken heads and silver bracts which make excellent indoor decoration.

S. smithii comes from the Falkland Islands and is fleshy in all its parts. The leaves are thick and dark on thick stems and the heads of white daisies look solid because the flowers are short-rayed. I grow it in the dampest part of the ditch under a north wall, where it looks comfortable and well favoured. But I will not pretend it has the fascination of S. pulcher which has something that takes it out of the category of ordinary plants. Its long leaves are dark and notched at the edges and covered with fine white hairs. The flowers are rosy pink daisies on rather a solid scale but by no means heavy. This plant flowers so late that it is seldom possible to get seed and as it does not seem to increase very fast I think it will always be rather scarce. It seems quite hardy but bad weather spoils the leaves and it needs protection if grown in exposed positions. I grow it in a narrow bed under an east wall, which is fairly damp.

Though astilbes will grow in an ordinary flower bed that is not too dry they do far better in a moist shady position. They look lovely growing by water where their delicate ferny foliage makes a needed contrast with the plants with big and solid leaves. Many have bronzed leaves in spring, others have foliage that is mahogany-coloured all through the season. I never cut down astilbes until the new growth appears in the spring because the stems and seed-heads turn a warm cigar brown which gives a glow of warmth throughout the winter.

Like so many other plants new varieties are introduced every year and for most of us they have to be admired but cannot be acquired. There is a limit to the number of astilbes one can grow in the garden and I, for one, would feel most ungrateful if I cast out my old friends when new arrivals came along. Of course, there are exceptions. *A.* 'Red Sentinel' is a real break with its intense scarlet-red flowers, and that has had to be squeezed in.

Of the named varieties *A.* 'Fanal' is, I think, still the best garnet and *A.* 'William Reeves' has bronze foliage as well as rose-crimson flowers. 'Apple Blossom' and 'Betsy Cuperus' are good pinks, 'Irrlicht' and 'Avalanche' white and 'King Albert' creamy white. 'Vesuvius' is the nearest to salmon and 'Amethyst' is lilac-purple. I have always grown the dumpy *A. chinensis pumila** for it makes excellent ground cover in damp, shady places and its foot-high flower spikes in mauvish pink are sturdy if not very striking. There is another called 'Perkeo' with pale pink flowers but it does not grow so well for me as the old commoner. Another dwarf which has white flowers is *A. simplicifolia*, with finely cut foliage in bronze tones, and *A. s. atrorosea*, which grows a little taller, has deep pink flowers grown rather loosely. *A. s.* 'Bronze Elegance' has bronze leaves with the pink flowers.

Several plants that used to be called spiraeas are now filipendulas. The tall deep pink *S. palmata* is now *Filipendula purpurea*. It is a tough plant with its 4-ft leafy stems and flat heads of tiny deep pink flowers. *F. hexapetala flore plena**, with pink-blushed buds and double cream flowers, makes good ground cover and does not demand such a damp position as some, but the double meadow sweet, *F. ulmaria*, and its golden form and the one with gold-variegated foliage are striking plants for damp shade, where they show up well. *F. rubra* has peach-coloured flowers, and *F. r. venusta** has flowers of deep pink.

An old-world plant that has roused public interest lately and is gradually getting back into circulation is the double form of *Ranunculus aconitifolius*, commonly known as Fair Maids of France—or of Kent, or white Bachelors' Buttons. It has beautifully cut buttercup leaves, which are dark and smooth, and many very double, very white little button flowers on branching stems. It disappears below ground after flowering, and can be increased by dividing its fleshy, claw-like roots, which are not unlike hosta roots. I have seen the single form of this plant once only and that is at Hidcote, in Gloucestershire. It is a much taller, thinner plant but attractive grown in a mass.

I grow the double buttercups in shade, though many people plant them in sun. My favourite is *R. carpaticus*, which I fondly cherished as the rare *R. bulbosus* until I asked an expert. But I am very pleased with it nevertheless, for it has wonderful buttercup leaves and large glistening yellow flowers with green centres. I like it much better than the running *R. speciosus plena**, with its smaller flowers, and *R. acris fl. pl**. which has small flowers too. Globe Flowers, trollius, love a damp position and if they have rich moist soil do not mind some shade. My own preference is always for species rather than hybrids and so I have great affection for the early *T. europaeus*, our native plant, with pale primrose flowers on 1 ½-ft stems. *T. 'Brynes Giant'** is lemon-yellow too and from there we get deeper and deeper in colour until we reach the richness of *T. 'Orange Queen'*. A recent introduction aptly named, *T. 'Alabaster'* was pale cream and a dream of gentle beauty but its delicacy was not confined to its colour. I was ashamed that I lost it several times but it was evidently not for this world for I see it has disappeared from most nurserymen's catalogues.

Lysimachia ephemerum is another plant that is becoming more popular in our quest for plants that are somewhat different. It is what I would call a back-room plant, not very outstanding in colour but a kind grey lady showing up the brilliant colours of other people. Its leaves are grey with a satin finish and sometimes show glints of green and bronze. Tiny pale grey flowers are clustered close to the long and graceful spikes, and later turn to attractive seed-heads.

The flowers of *L. clethroides* are white and shaped like a shepherd's crook, and I like to plant the clumps with their backs to a wall or taller shrubs so that all the crooks face the same way. It will grow in an ordinary bed that does not get too dry, and though it increases with long, pink-flushed roots, which can be detached and will each grow into a plant, they do have the decency to remain anchored to a centre crown instead of running hither and thither at a terrific speed as do the roots of *L. punctata*, with its whorled yellow flowers. Even a dry position does not discourage its antics, but it is an excellent subject for filling in any waste spots, and there are two better forms, *L. ciliosa**, which is more branching in habit and the

1. *Rheum palmatum* in the Lido Ditch

2. *Rosa mundi* in the Terraces

3. A shady path in the Terraces

4. Climbing *Rosa* 'Iceberg' flowering well under *Prunus subtirhella* 'Autumnalis'

5. *Lysichytum americanum* dominates mixed planting in the Lido Ditch

6. The Ditch in late spring

7. Astrantia, geraniums and valerian in semi-shade

8. *Rosa filipes* 'Kiftsgate' flourishing up an old apple tree

9. *Primula japonica* happy in damp shade

10. Variegated knotweed (*Fallopia japonica* 'Variegata')
best without direct sunlight

11. East end of the Lido Ditch in early 1960s

12. View towards the north side of the house

13. *Cornus mas* 'Variegata' in the White Garden, which is now very shady

14. *Acer pseudoplatynus* 'Leopoldii' dominates the front lawn

15. The Ditch behind the Malthouse looking north

16. Further along the Ditch behind the Malthouse

17. Shade in the Terraces beneath *Rhus potaninii* and *Syringa emodii* 'Variegata'

18. *Hedera helix* 'Buttercup' on the east wall of the Malthouse

19. The Ditch in early spring

20. Attractive form of *Weigelia florida* 'Variegata' flowering well in semi-shade

21. *Cornus controversa* 'Variegata' with clematis in full shade

22. The magnificent *Acer pseudoplatynus* 'Leopoldii' seen as visitors enter the garden

23. *Oxalis trifoliata* as ground cover in the shade

24. The Silver Garden viewed from the White Garden in shade

25. A purple hazel (*Corylus maxima* 'Purpurea') dominates the north end of the Terraces

26. *Ranunculus flore pleno* in the Ditch

27. Silver and grey plants can also flourish in semi-shade

28. The Terraces viewed from under the acer on the front lawn

29. Many old-fashioned roses give months of interest in semi-shade on the Strip

30. An unidentified tree peony flowering happily in the shade

orange-eyed *L. ocelata*. Creeping Jenny, *L. nummularia* is always willing to oblige and it soon covers any moist soil with its shining green leaves. *L. n. aurea** with golden leaves is particularly useful for dark corners.

One has only to admire the ordinary loosestrife, *Lythrum salicaria*, growing in damp ditches in our hedgerows to realise that its cultivated forms are lovely for a damp position. There are several good named varieties in bright rose-red, and they seed themselves liberally so one gets all shades of deep pink and mauve-pink. I grew some from seed years ago, laboriously tending the little ones on bits of damp flannel, which I was told was the way to do it, but I don't think I need have taken so much trouble as I get all the seedlings I want in my damp, shady ditch, with no help from me at all. The *Lythrum virgatum* variations are different in growth, having slightly running roots and many spikes of small bright pink flowers, and they are dwarfer plants. *L. v.* 'Rose Queen' is the one most usually grown.

There are quite a number of irises which will grow in damp shade. The tallest is *I. ochroleuca**, which grows to 4 ft and has very good sword-like leaves. It has white flowers with yellow falls, and *I. ochraurea** has yellow flowers, with deeper yellow markings.

Though it is usually recommended that *I. sibirica* should be grown in sun, I grow mine in the shade of the ditch and they grow and flower remarkably well. The blues range from a pale blue-grey through the China blue of 'Perry's Blue' to the deep Oxford blue of 'Mrs Saunders'. 'Caesar' and 'Emperor' are violet, and 'Eric the Red' is the reddest. My favourite is 'Snow Queen'*, which I grow in a dark damp corner, where it shows up well.

I. laevigata likes to grow very near if not actually right in the water, and does not mind shade. I once saw a huge planting of the variegated form in a pond under trees. The old rose *I. l.* 'Rose Queen'* is an unusual shade for an iris and very pleasant and there is a lovely white form. This iris does not like lime and though I can keep it in my limy clay it doesn't increase much.

Another damp-loving iris which I grow in shade is *I. setosa*, both deep blue and crimson, and, of course, the common yellow flag *I. pseudacorus* will grow anywhere that is damp. I am not averse to the ordinary wild type, but find its seeding habits a little trying. The form with primrose-coloured flowers is definitely worth growing and there is one with variegated leaves, which is very striking in the spring. Like some others among variegated plants the leaves turn green in late summer, and you wonder if you have the right plant.

The two plants with uliginosa after their names of course like to grow in damp places. *Salvia uliginosa* has most beautiful Cambridge blue flowers and does quite well in a shady place. Though the white chrysanthemum Moon Daisy will grow anywhere it needs rather a damp place to reach its maximum height of

5 ft. A true cottage garden plant I doubt if this stalwart appears in many nurserymen's lists nowadays, which is a pity, because it is a reliable, likeable plant and has only the fault of growing too lustily. I grow it in shade and I know several cottage gardens where there are flourishing plantings in the shade of old apple trees.

The primulas that like a damp position are among the loveliest plants we grow. They come in every flower colour except blue, and who knows, we may have a blue candelabra primula one of these days. All they need is shade and a soil that is damp but does not become sodden or sour. Left to themselves they will seed prolifically and can also be divided in spring.

The drumstick primulas, *P. denticulata*, are easy to grow and very effective in the garden, with their round heads and pale crinkled leaves. The colours range from soft lavender to deep lilac, and there are also white and ruby-red forms. *P. d. cachemiriana** has smaller flowers in rather a slaty mauve, with dark eyes, and grey-green leaves. It is a quiet and restrained plant, what one would call well-bred in a human.

These primulas can be increased by seed or by root cuttings. The orthodox way to take these is, of course, to lift the plants and cut pieces of root about an inch long, being careful to make on one end a slanting cut and a straight one to the other so that they are planted the right way up. An easy way of increasing the plants is to take a sharp trowel and scoop out a plant leaving the ends of the roots in the ground. The poor maimed plant will grow quite well if replanted in a mixture of sand, peat and loam, and the same mixture is used to put in the hole from which the plant was taken. The bits of root left in the soil should sprout and soon become nice little plants.

There is an air of abundance about *P. japonica*, the large crinkled leaves are generous and the tiers of bright flowers rise on stout stems. The prevailing colour is rather a magenta-red, but among the named varieties there are 'Miller's Crimson' and 'Postford White'. I have never been able to keep the latter and it must be rather casual in its mating for some of its progeny are as piebald as a mongrel cat. *P.* 'Rowallane Rose' is a beautiful shade of pink which comes from that famous Irish garden.

In *P. pulverulenta* the stems are thickly powdered and the normal flowers are purplish red with a darker eye. But the Bartley strain of these mealy-stemmed primulas includes some lovely shades of soft pink and pale salmon. There are two strains of candelabra primulas which include many shades of yellow, apricot, flame and salmon-pink. *P.* 'Lissadel' hybrids is one, and in the other, *P.* 'Asthore', which is raised from *P. bulleyana*, occasional mauve and purple flowers occur. The crimson flowers of *P. beesiana* are scented, and in *P. burmanica* there are yellow eyes to the reddish purple flowers.

The tallest of the yellow primulas and also the most robust is *P. florindae*. It flowers late and wafts its scent upon the air for some distance around. It is completely deciduous and has very fine red roots, but its leaves are broad and almost heart-shaped. I have never had much success with the golden yellow *P. helodoxa** but another yellow primula, *P. prolifera* (an improved form of *P. helodoxa*), grows well for me. It has a silver sheen to its big and crumpled leaves and the flowers are a clear, cool yellow. There are lovely cream primulas, the pale *chionantha* which is scented and nearly white, and *P. sikkimensis*, the Himalayan cowslip, with nodding scented flowers.

When a stronger colour is needed *P. bulleyana*, another candelabra type with burnt orange flowers is not difficult to please. One of the most unusual of the primulas is also one of the most difficult to keep. *P. vialii* looks like a small kniphofia with spikes of violet flowers made dazzling by scarlet calyces.

The brilliant carmine pink of *P. rosea* is best grown against a green background. It is almost piercing in its intensity, but it can be lovely so long as there is no yellow or orange in the vicinity. It is exciting when its buds of sealing-wax-red first appear, to be followed by bronze-tinged leaves

The monkey flowers, mimulus, like shade and moisture, though *M. cardinalis* in shades of red and yellow is not so in insistent on moisture as *M. luteus*. The best form of this is that attributed to the late A. T. Johnson, and has crimson blotches on the petals. *M. cupreus* 'Red Emperor'* and 'Whitecroft Scarlet' are quite dwarf but the rose-pink *M. lewisii*, with pointed hairy leaves, grows to 18 in. There is an interesting double musk, *M. luteus duplex**, in yellow and bronze.

Double cardamines, with pale lavender flowers and marsh marigolds are good dwarf plants. The white marsh marigold, *Caltha palustris alba**, is very early and rather smaller than the yellow one, just as the double golden marsh marigold is smaller than the single one. *C. polypetala** is a handsome, very full kingcup.

The willows, of course, are happy in shade, and need a moist soil. The weeping willow, *Salix vitellina pendula**, with its golden bark, particularly. *S. alba argentea** is a beautiful small tree, growing to about 12 ft, with silvery, silken leaves, and the twisted willow, *S. matsudana tortuosa**, which hasn't a straight stem or leaf about it, is particularly lovely when silhouetted against the wintry sky.

Bamboos like to grow in damp shady places and are quite happy under taller shrubs. Some, of course, are too rampant except where thick cover is needed, but there are others which can be admitted even to a small garden. The most beautiful is *Arundinaria nitida**, with slender purple-black canes and small dark leaves. *A. murielae** has yellow stems and very narrow leaves, and in *A. japonica** the stems are pale grey-green, with dark glossy foliage. *A. pumila* is an interesting pygmy which makes stocky little clumps of dark green about a foot high. The lovely golden bamboo, *A. auricoma**, needs a sunny position to keep its colour, but the various small silver-variegated types grow well in shade.

~ 8 ~
Rock Gardens

Most rock gardens are made in full sun, and yet very few mountain plants grow where they do not get a certain amount of shade each day, unless they come from high southern slopes. As a rough guess I should say there are more rock plants that will grow in shade than those that insist on a sunny site. This is certainly so with ericaceous plants; acid soil and shade seem to go together. Making a shady rock garden on alkaline soil may need a little more thought, but there is no lack of material.

The campanulas are a great standby; they like lime, they are quite happy in shade and there are a great many of them. The two rampers are better in walls or covering banks unless the rock garden is very big. *C. portenschlagiana* is the more modest of the two but it is very persistent and though it does not send out the long trails of *C. poscharskyana* it has great underground ramifications and is difficult to eradicate when once it takes hold. *C. garganica* is not unlike *C. portenschlagiana* but it is more modest and no one would mind its neat clumps of starry-eyed blue flowers. The white form of *C. poscharskyana* is not quite so rampant as the blue one, or is it more unusual and we do not mind it spreading itself? The pink form is not too bad either but its colour is washy and I would not bother with it if I had not plenty of room.

There are many campanulas of the harebell type, *C. cochlearifolia*, *C. pulla* and *C. x pulloides*. They all increase quietly but never enough to be a nuisance. Put them at one end of a long paving crack and they will work away steadily until they fill it. They come in shades of blue and in white and are dainty little plants small enough for a trough but sufficiently determined to hold their own anywhere. There are several named varieties such as *C. x hallii* in white, 'Miss Willmott' a good medium blue, and 'Oakington Blue' a much deeper shade. I was given a small white campanula, as *C.* 'Covadonga' but the experts give the colour as blue, so it may not be correct.

C. planiflora alba* is one of my favourite campanulas, with its neat rosettes of dark green and stiff 6-in spikes of white flowers. Though the white form pleases me most the porcelain-blue *C. planiflora caerulea** is a very close second. *C. carpatica* grows to about 9 in so it is too big for a trough but useful in a good-sized rock garden and excellent in paving that is in shade and will not be walked on. I still like the rich blue *C. carpatica* 'Isobel best', but there are more than a dozen varieties to choose from including two white ones, 'Bressingham White' and 'White Star', and 'Blue Moonlight', pale blue at its most refined.

C. isophylla is usually associated with hanging baskets, and the white form trails from low containers on window sills. I think the blue *C. isophylla* is quite hardy, and I know gardens near London where it does well. I grow it to hang down over a low wall which has a large *Euphorbia wulfenii** shading it, and though it does not increase much it remains with me. Now I am trying the variegated form, *C. i. mayi**, which most people grow in pans in the cold greenhouse. The white isophylla is definitely not hardy. I have tried it in several parts of the garden and each winter sees the end of it, and yet it grows well in a garden not far from me but not quite in the open. There are troughs standing against the house walls but with a glass roof above, which gives the campanula the protection it needs.

There are many more campanulas from which to choose. *C.* 'Lynchmere' is rather unusual, with grey-green leaves and deep slate-blue flowers, and *C.* x *stansfieldii** with violet flowers on 4-in stems.

Several little irises refused to grow for me when I grew them in full sun but succeeded when I found them shady homes. *I. cristata* not only wanted shade but a lime-free soil as well, and now in greensand it increases well and produces plenty of its lilac-blue flowers. There is also a white form. *I. gracilipes*, with lavender, gold-crested flowers needs the same shady, peaty conditions. The white form is lovely but rare and expensive. *I. lacustris* is usually considered a form of *I. cristata* but it seems difficult to believe because instead of peat it does best in a gritty soil and with me it has settled down in a shady spot at the edge of the path. Here it increases and produces its perfect iris flowers in mauve, with golden crests, on 3-in stalks, at odd times over a long period.

Another plant that blooms on and off for many weeks is *Omphalodes cappadocica*. Shade and moisture are its requirements and perched between stones on the lower slopes of the rock garden it makes a big clump of pointed leaves with showers of gentian-blue flowers for weeks on end. *O. verna* has blue flowers too but I do not find it nearly such a neat and reliable plant and I think it should take its long arms and wandering ways to a woodland planting where it could sprawl to its heart's content. At its best it is a straggling plant, and the rough hairy leaves are not nearly so enjoyable as those of *O. cappadocica*. But it flowers very early in the year and has a white counterpart, which is less straggling in growth.

I realise I shall shock many people when I recommend growing *O. luciliae* in lime-free soil in shade. I have tried it in all parts of the garden but it was only when I broke all the rules that I had any success. My change of heart came after I had seen a magnificent specimen growing between stones in a wall facing north in the garden of a friend. There were hellebores behind it and trees above it and its beautiful blue-grey leaves made a swirl a foot deep down the wall. It seeds itself in the ground below and produces many pale blue flowers, some of which have a suspicion of pink. I know that the accepted place for this plant is in a trough in full sun with a stone over its roots, but I copied my friend and tried my next *O. luciliae* in a sunless spot in greensand under a north wall. It worked and now I have another little plant growing well in a similar spot.

Many of the aquilegias like to grow in sun, but there are two rock garden types that enjoy a shady site. *Aquilegia bertolinii** with its flowers of deep blue and white is a most unusual little plant, with a nice clean look about it. *A. viridiflora* is that shade of sea-green that is almost blue. It is difficult to buy as a plant but is easily grown from seed.

An unusual and delightful plant for spring flowering is orobus (more correctly known as lathyrus), a dwarf pea-flowered plant growing about 9 in high with dainty, fern-like foliage. I think the prettiest is *L. vernus albo-roseus**, with salmon-pink and white flowers. *L. vernus* itself is bluish purple or purplish blue, with a suggestion of crimson about it. There is a form with brilliant blue flowers, *L. cyaneus*, which comes from Persia, and another with white flowers. I notice that some books recommend this for sun but I grow mine in shade and find they do well and sometimes seed. Ordinary white arabis is best grown in walls or on rough banks where it can spread as much as it likes but there is a fairly compact form called 'Snowflake' that can be grown in a rock garden that is not too small. The pink varieties, *A. muralis** and *A. albida rosa-bella**, are not too spreading, but the best of the lot is the double white arabis, which has sturdy spikes of double white flowers and looks like a dwarf stock. Another white flower which will grow in shade is perennial candytuft. *Iberis saxatilis* is the smallest, growing to 2 to 3 in only, *I. sempervirens* 'Little Gem' is a little bigger and about 6 in high, while *I. s.* 'Snowflake' has large white flowers and is about a foot high.

When I started gardening I planted the paving in front of my rock gardens with 'Dresden China' daisies and they did very well for a time, but very few of my original plantings are left now. They liked the cool root run between the stones but not the hot position in full sun. If I watered them regularly they might have prospered, and they need good rich living to do well. I don't plant them in the sun any more but find nice shady places under shrubs or tall perennials. The spaces between the stones are now filled with *Gentiana acaulis*, but even these are bigger and more likely to flower if they get a bit of shade from something taller (which ought not to be there). Daisies, I find, tuck themselves under taller plants if they can and I can always count on good plants of the dark red 'Rob Roy' under a *Mahonia japonica* and under a *Viburnum fragrans** in another part of the garden. I would like to have them in a sunny border but they refuse to grow there, and the miserable, woody specimens are hardly recognisable beside the big, luxuriant plants growing in the shade. Many people cannot keep *Bellis* 'Dresden China' and I am sure the reason is that they are grown in sun and are not divided regularly. When I have a particularly difficult subject, like the white form of 'Dresden China', I plant it in shade in deep, rich soil and put stones over its roots. Recently I was given *B.* 'Alice', the pink form of 'Rob Roy' who has been in hiding for some years and evaded us all. It now grows in a shaded gully between walls and has a barricade of stones to keep its roots cool.

The Hen and Chickens Daisy is a proliferous form which is not difficult to keep if it is planted in rich soil in light shade, and divided regularly. This plant is my 'fancy-work' in the garden. When I have a few minutes to spare and want to enjoy myself I lift, divide and replant several clumps of this daisy, and feel very much better. It grows in a bed shaded by a rosemary and a *Buddleia alternifolia*, and I know that as long as I divide, feed, shade and water the plants I shall have a flourishing colony of this old plant.

Given a start between stones in a moist position *Arenaria balearica* will soon cover the soil around and work its way up the sides of stones in any shady corner. I have never found *Arenaria montana* or *A. purpurascens* easy to keep. Both can be grown in a shady rock garden but *A. montana* does not do well in a shade that is too dense.

Androsaces are good plants for shade and they enjoy themselves if they can send down runners, with little tufts attached, to be anchored wherever they may touch the ground. *A. sarmentosa* and *A. mucronifolia* (*A. microphylla*) are good at this game and they like to play it on a bank. The former has greyish tufts and rose-pink flowers. In the latter case the rosettes are smaller and the rose-pink flowers are in proportion.

Though the asperulas like shade they do not enjoy winter rain and to keep them happy they need a pane of glass over their heads in winter. *A. gussonii**, *lilaciflora caespitosa**, and *suberosa* are all good species with flowers in various shades of pink. The astilbes, of course, like as much moisture as possible and the dwarf *A. chinensis*, with its rosy-purple flower spikes and the pinky-white *A. simplicifolia* do best in shade in as moist a position as possible.

Nothing is more beautiful in autumn than the creeping *Ceratostigma plumbaginoides*, a dwarf hardy plumbago, and it is happy in light shade. The flowers are the most brilliant blue imaginable, and when in October the leaves turn scarlet the effect is really sumptuous. It makes a good contrast to a silver background such as is supplied by *Artemisia lanata** (*A. pedemontana*), which grows happily in shade.

Hepaticas used to be called *Anemone hepatica* but for once the higher-ups have simplified a name. Flowering in February and March they need shade, a deep root

run, and hate to be disturbed. Most of them do best in a moist peaty soil but
H. transsilvanica is less particular if one's soil is chalky. It has sky-blue flowers and
grey-green leaves, and there is an outstanding form called *H.* x *ballardii**, with
much bigger flowers and a more erect habit of growth. *H. lilacina** has lilac-pink
flowers and *H.* 'Loddon Blue' medium blue flowers. *H. triloba** offers the most
variations. It has larger, more glossy leaves and flowers that may be blue, white or
pink. There are also double pink and double blue varieties but they are rare and not
very easy to find.

Some of the saxifrage family are definitely plants for shade, the mossy varieties
do   not   like   being   exposed   to   blazing   sun,   and   the   varieties   of
S. oppositifolia are always happiest in a damp shady crevice, such as is provided by
deep stones. The tiny *S. umbrosa* 'Elliott's Variety'*, with dainty spikes of pink
flowers, likes to ramble along a shady rock ledge. Ordinary London Pride,
S. umbrosa, is useful for edging shady beds, planted with ferns and shrubs, but some
of the varieties can be used in the rock garden. *S. u. melvillei** is good for dry shade,
S. u. 'Geum'* will grow in any shady spot and turns bright red in winter, and *S. u.*
'Inglesborough', with its finely scalloped edges, will grow in any shady spot, but is
slow to increase. The variegated London Pride, *S. u. variegata**, with its glints of gold
and touches of pink in winter, does best in shade. The other saxifrages, for the most
part, need sun as well as gritty soil and sharp drainage, but they will stand the shade
from overhanging rocks, which is what they would get in nature.

S. fortunei is one of the greatest thrills of the autumn. It is rather large for the
average rock garden, although I think a foot-high plant among so many very small
ones makes a pleasant break. It needs shade and moisture and is happy in a
woodland setting, where its hovering white flowers dance above shiny bronze
leaves which are lined with crimson. Wada's form has particularly rich red leaves
and this is the one we all try to get, but it is not as quick growing as the normal
variety, or so it seems to me.

No one could consider a shady rock garden without cyclamen and these
provide flowers or leaves, and sometimes both, throughout the year. All through
the winter the various forms of *C. orbiculatum** give white, pink and crimson
flowers, in spring there is *C. repandum*, then we have *C. cilicium*, to be followed by
the scented *C. europaeum**. And while that is still blooming *C. neapolitanum** will
start, with flowers of white or pink. The leaves appear in early autumn and stay as
handsome ground cover until early summer, with occasional flowers among them
until November and December.

Most people grow the blue anemones, *A. blanda*, which can also be pink, and *A.
apennina*, which can be white or double, but not so often the delightful little wood
anemone, *A. nemorosa*, which likes a heavy soil as well as shade. The double white

form looks like a tiny rose and there is another form with a ruff of green leaves behind its head. *A. n. allenii** is lavender-blue, *A. n.* 'Blue Bonnet' is deep blue, and *A. n. robinsoniana** lavender-blue within and white without. *A. obtusiloba patula** looks like a blue buttercup both in flower and leaf. To show what it can do it should be planted in shade.

For the adventurous there are several interesting little calceolarias that demand light moist soil in shade but can be difficult even when all their requirements are fulfilled. *C. darwinii* has to be seen to be believed, with its top-heavy golden pouches marked with brown and having a white bar across the centre. *C. biflora* has twin pouches in yellow and in *C. polyrrhiza** the gold is flecked with purple.

Much easier and more useful when it is a question of covering the ground are the dwarf dicentras which need shade but not a very wet soil. The most beautiful, I think, is *D. eximia alba**, with its panicles of pure white flowers but others may prefer the pink. *D. formosa*, or its deeper pink form *D. f.* 'Bountiful', which lives up to its name.

Primroses and polyanthus are rather large for a rock garden but the tiny varieties of primula are lovely tucked against stones. One of the smallest is the brick-red *P.* 'E. R. Janes', and the tiny polyanthus-type 'Lady Greer' in deep ivory, and its soft pink counterpart. The pale pink-lavender *P. altaica* (*vulgaris rubra*)* is one of the first to flower, and for richness of colour *P.* 'Wisley Red' with flat crinkled red leaves and deep crimson flowers is not difficult to please. All the farinosae primulas like a moist, shady position. *P. clarkei* is small, with tiny rose-pink flowers and coppery crimson leaves. For me it grows best in a lime-free bed, but other people may find it easy anywhere. The powdered *P. farinosa*, with lilac flowers, and *P. frondosa*, with a distinct yellow eye to its rosy lilac flowers, are not difficult, and the bright pink *P. rosea* needs a really moist position.

The petiolares primulas are not easy south of the Border, although they do well in the Savill Gardens at Windsor and in Devonshire. They need a sunless position that is not too dry and are happiest if the soil is constantly brought up and packed close to their crowns. One can do that but it is not possible to give them the soft moist air they like and though the lovely *P. bhutanica** and the pretty pink *P. gracilipes* may last a season or two a very dry summer will usually see the end of them. The pubescens primulas are easier and if they are planted in shade with stones at their backs or over their roots they seldom look back. I grow mine in stone troughs which they seem to like. The rich lavender 'Mrs J. H. Wilson' is one of the best, and there is a rare white form, *P.* x *pubescens alba**.

One always connects yellow flowers with sunshine but there are some that like shade. *Waldsteinia ternata* might easily be taken for a buttercup, for its leaves are similar, but it has golden flowers that hang in bunches and makes a thick carpet by overground stems. It does very well in the dry soil under trees where it will produce odd flowers throughout the summer after its big display in spring. *Patrinia triloba* (*P. palmata*) is a Japanese plant with particularly attractive glossy leaves and golden flowers in late summer. *Chrysogonum virginianum* is often grown in sun but it is just as happy in shade. It grows about 9 in high and produces its yellow flowers on and off most of the summer. *Oxalis valdiviensis* sows itself in shade as often as in sun. It is a neat little plant with yellow flowers which needs only to be planted in the garden once for it to go on reappearing every year.

Haberleas and ramondas do not need a lime-free soil but they must have shade and do best when leaf-mould is added to the soil. There is an idea that they must be grown in a vertical position on a north-facing wall or bank. The aspect need not necessarily be north, though this is the most sunless, and though they do very well in an upright position in a wall they do just as well on a shallow slope between stones. *Ramonda myconi* (*R. pyrenaica*) is a soft lilac-blue, *R. m. rosea** has delicate peach-pink flowers, and there is also a white form. The lavender haberlea is *H. rhodopensis*, and there is an entrancing white one, *H. r. virginalis**.

Tiny plants that carpet odd corners can be useful and for this any of the low-growing linarias are good. *L. aequitriloba** is very dwarf and *L. alpina* in violet or pink grows to 3 in. *Pratia treadwellii** needs a damp position and does not mind shade. Its small lobelia-like flowers are followed by purple berries, sometimes both appearing at the same time, and *Hypsella longiflora**, has mauve or white flowers all through the summer, and also likes rather a moist position. The prostrate *Mazus reptans* has bronze leaves and mauve, white and gold-flecked flowers all through the summer.

With a lime-free soil there is no difficulty in finding plants that like shade. So often sun and lime go together and an acid soil conjures up pictures of shade. First of all there are the gentians; they do best in a shady spot, they all need plenty of moisture and, with the exception of the two easy ones, *G. septemfida* and *G. lagodechiana**, they all do best in a heavy peaty soil, even the problem child *G. acaulis*, which is often so difficult to flower. I have seen it growing happily in peat walls, working its way in and out of the blocks, making enormous leaves and producing twice as many much larger flowers. The autumn-flowering gentians— *G. sino-ornata*, *G. farreri*, *G. macaulayi** and *G. newberryi*, among others—of course need damp shade in lime-free soil, and then they race away.

Phlox adsurgens does not succeed for everyone but that may be a matter of sun and lime. Grow it in shade in lime-free soil and it will produce its lovely salmon-pink flowers with great generosity. I would give the same treatment to *P. stolonifera* 'Blue Ridge', which can sometimes be difficult.

The blue shamrock pea, *Parochetus communis*, needs shade and though it may struggle along in a limy soil, it loses all restraint in peat walls and beds and will go on producing its brilliant blue flowers until Christmas. Blue flowers seem to go with lime-free soil. There is *Cyananthus integer**, with large powder-blue flowers at the ends of its long and slender stems. It is often blooming at the same time as the sino-ornata type gentians and likes the same conditions. *Penstemon heterophyllus* 'True Blue' is another blue flower which can sometimes be tiresome, in fact, I could never keep it until I put it in a lime-free bed under a north wall and now it goes on year after year. The most startling blue of all is *Corydalis cashmeriana*. It is the most intense blue, almost metallic, in its purity and with a suggestion of green, particularly in the early stages, with typical fern-like leaves, and I spent a small fortune on plants until I discovered the remedy was shade and no lime. The other members of the corydalis family like shade, but will grow in any soil.

For anyone with a shady rock garden on lime-free soil there are two wonderful plants to grow, shortias and schizocodon. They need to be planted in a position where the sun can never reach them, and then, if the soil is right, they increase well and flower regularly. The rounded shiny leaves are beautifully shaped and have in them many hints of red. The hanging flowers can be pink or white and either frilled or fringed.

Jeffersonia dubia is always spoken about with great respect but it is not really a difficult plant if it is planted in the right place, which is in shade and in lime-free soil. Once established it comes up regularly year after year and for two weeks and more one enjoys its delicate fluttering flowers. They are rather like anemones in a round open shape, in pale lavender, and the leaves are rounded too. I was given *J. diphylla*, which is talked about with even more respect, but it did not trouble to put up a leaf the following year. I was most distressed but friends tell me that I need not grieve too much because *J. dubia* is by far the better plant. Jeffersonias disappear underground after flowering so it is important to plant them in a place where they will not be disturbed.

Another plant which likes the same kind of treatment is *Glaucidium palmatum*. This is really a woodland plant but I would not like to risk its pale loveliness in a wild garden which can become a jungle after a few weeks of neglect. Only 12 in high it is not too large for the rock garden, where it should be planted in a position where it can be admired but not disturbed. It has maple-like leaves and flowers of lustrous lavender which are rather like poppies in shape.

Lithospermums are among the easiest plants if they have the right conditions. Then they turn themselves into heavy mats of dark green foliage with brilliant blue flowers that come and go most of the summer. *L. diffusum* 'Grace Ward'* and 'Heavenly Blue'* are the two most usually grown. The rampant *L. purpureo-*

*caeruleum** is a wonderful plant for covering large areas but it is not safe to let it loose in a rock garden and it does not mind lime.

For many a long year I struggled with the polygalas and it was only when I planted them in shade in lime-free soil that they started to grow. They make neat little shrubs about 6 in high and have dark and glossy evergreen foliage. *P. chamaebuxus* has little pea flowers in white and yellow and *P. purpurea** and *P. vayredae* have purple and yellow flowers.

Dwarf shrubs help a rock garden. They give it substance and prevent that flimsy look which results from too many small subjects planted far apart. *Gaultheria cuneata* never grows more than 12 in but it spreads over the years and intermingles with other plants. It is evergreen and its leathery leaves turn scarlet in winter. White bell flowers turn to pink-flushed white berries, which last for many weeks. *Gaulnettya* 'Wisley Pearl'* is taller and grows to 12 to 15 in. It too spreads a bit and its waxy white flowers turn to rich red berries.

There is no more beautiful shrub for early spring than *Daphne blagayana*. It needs shade but is not so insistent on lime-free soil as the two shrubs I have just mentioned. But it needs room to thrust out its long stems that will produce those deliciously scented cream flowers, and to keep it happy flat stones should be placed on top of the soil that covers them. I find *D. cneorum eximia** is very happy in a shady spot, but it is more fussy about soil, which it prefers without lime.

~ 9 ~

Annuals

Although nearly all annual plants do best in sun there are enough that will flower quite well in shade to decorate a shady garden. Inevitably there are spaces between shrubs or larger perennials where annuals are needed and by choosing the right ones the garden can be as gay in the summer as any sunny one.

One would not expect red flax, *Linum grandiflorum*, to be happy in shade but a friend of mine with a very shady garden grows it regularly and finds that it looks even richer in shade than in full sun, and, of course, flowers for a very long time. There is a new variety which is an improvement on the ordinary plant. *L. g.* 'Venice Red' has particularly large flowers of brilliant carmine-scarlet, with a silky sheen on the petals. Patches in shady borders rustle gently as they sway in the breeze.

Phacelia campanularia is another deep-toned annual that is good in shade and which blends well with shrubs. I never think that strong contrast is nearly as satisfying as a subtle blending, and for this there are several phacelias which can be used. *P. parryi* has purplish blue bell-shaped flowers, in *P. tanacetifolia* the lavender flowers are crowded on the stems, while *P. viscida* 'Musgrave Strain' has white centres to its dark blue flowers, which one would expect in a plant grown by the late Gertrude Jekyll.

Love in a Mist (*Nigella damascena*) seeds itself all over my garden and I find it in many shady corners. I expect in the first place I grew *N. damascena* 'Miss Jekyll', which is a good form with large bright blue flowers. Miss Jekyll is supposed to be responsible for another in intense deep blue, and certainly for the pure white form, as she loved white flowers. *N. hispanica* comes from Spain and is sometimes called Fennel Flower. It is quite distinct and is upright in growth and has dark green leaves with large scented flowers which have a cluster of dark red stamens in the centre.

When an occasional plant of honesty is allowed to run its full course and discard its outer discs so that the silvered moons are left, the effect against a dark background is dazzling. In the hushed atmosphere of a woodland planting or among shrubs the plants rustle and shimmer mysteriously but their dry stems are brittle and they must have shelter if they are to last. When starting honesty in the garden it is pleasant to grow as many variations as possible from seed. Again Miss Jekyll is supposed to be responsible for the pure white-flowered form, *Lunaria annua alba**, and the deep purple *L. a.* 'Munstead Purple'. The interesting variegated honesty has crimson flowers.

I always plant carpets of dwarf annuals between shrubs and tall perennials, starting with a patch of five or seven near the front of the bed and tapering them off to wander way into the undergrowth. The various coloured forms of *Lobelia erinus*, which is grown as an annual, are excellent grown like this and look so different that they sometimes mystify other gardeners. My favourite is *L. e.* 'Cambridge Blue', or other shades of blue, 'Opal', 'Blue Stone' and 'Blue Gown'; there are also others with crimson, wine or white flowers. *Limanthes douglasii* sows itself regularly for me, very often in shady places and is particularly good under trees and shrubs where its white, golden-centred flowers last for many weeks. Its country name is Custard and Cream and it is attractive to bees. *Crepis rubra* looks rather like a dandelion to the unwary but when it flowers the double-shaded pink flowers are quite distinct. *Omphalodes linifolia* (Venus' Navel Wort) is also a neat little plant with glaucous leaves, like the aristocratic *O. lucilae*, but with white flowers. Sweet alyssum will put up with a certain amount of shade and sows itself regularly every year in shade as well as sun. There are several good named varieties of this annual alyssum, *Lobularia maritima* (*Alyssum maritimum*), in shades of pink as well as lilac and violet, e.g. 'Lilac Queen', 'Pink Heather', etc.

Asperula orientalis (*A. azurea*) is a scented lavender-blue form of our native woodruff. It is not as dwarf as some of the other annuals mentioned nor is *Cerinthe aspera**, a member of the borage family with flowers that are yellow in the lower half and brownish purple above. There is a wallflower which is quite a good shade plant: *Erysimum perofskianum*, with deep orange flowers growing to 1 ½ ft.

A little plant to grow among light or silver foliage is commonly known as *Viola* 'Bowles Black'*. Once a seedling comes into the garden it will keep itself going but not all the flowers could be called black, in fact, with me, many are a very deep blue. It is a perky little plant, never a nuisance and so neat and unassuming that one has not the heart to pull out chance seedlings, even if they are in the wrong place.

There is a small pink oxalis which makes a charming carpet under trees and keeps its looks for a very long time. I first saw it growing under a large spreading tree in Mrs Fleischmann's lovely garden at Batsford, in the Cotswolds. She told me that it had come from Mr Clarence Elliott. Not being able to find out anything about it or its name, I wrote to Mr Elliott and he confirms that it is *Oxalis rosea**, but he says: 'I must confess that I am very uncertain about that name. I found the plant carpeting a spinney of giant pines in South Chile and collected a little seed, which I sowed under a pine at my nursery at Stevenage, where it colonised and flourished. I fancy it is little more than an annual anyway, the plants die in any normal English winter and seedlings come up the following spring and it never seemed to stray from the host pine'.

The feathery foliage that surrounds the crimson flowers of *Adonis aestivalis* makes a contrast to straight sword-like leaves of iris or sisyrinchium, and against very dark, solid leaves I would suggest *Hunnemannia fumariifolia* 'Sunlite', with its delicate silvery grey leaves and bright yellow poppy flowers. It is a bushy plant about 1 ½ ft high.

Strangely enough the rather fleshy *Calandrina discolor*, which has bright purplish flowers will grow in shade. It has conspicuous yellow stamens which show up well under shrubs. *Layia elegans**, commonly known as 'tidy tips', is a neat scented daisy about the same height, with white-tipped yellow petals round a darker disc centre.

Nasturtiums (Tropaeolum) are marvellous annuals for shade. Put a few seedlings of any of the many varieties available in a shady corner and by the end of the summer it will be solid with beautiful leaves and flowers. The trailers work down banks and the climber, *T. peregrinum* (canary creeper), will cover walls and fences and clamber over any plant in the vicinity without doing any damage.

It is not necessary to grow only the fiery orange which one connects with all nasturtiums, the flowers can be primrose or yellow, maroon or deep velvety crimson, pink or salmon, with single or double flowers. The 'Tom Thumb' varieties are good in small spaces and variation of foliage is another way of adding interest. The dark leaves of *T.* 'Empress of India' show up the deep crimson flowers as do those of 'Black Beauty' and 'Fire Cloth', and they are dark, with salmon-rose flowers in *T.* 'Vesuvius'. I was once given a precious nasturtium with a variegated leaf and tried to over-winter it indoors as one does the double orange nasturtium, I didn't succeed and then discovered with joy that I could buy seed, which I now do every year. In the 'Queen of Tom Thumb Mixed'* the flowers may be various colours with silver-variegated leaves, but in 'Queen of T. T. Ryburgh Perfection'* one knows that the flowers are scarlet, with the same variegated leaves. Some of the present-day nasturtiums are scented and many will sow themselves year after year if allowed to seed.

Foliage plants are always helpful and for this the rich crimson leaves of *Atriplex hortensis cupreata** bring glowing colour into the garden, and are particularly lovely in the early evening when the rays of the setting sun shine through them. The leaves have a purple bloom which shows up well against dark violet stems. They are good for picking and so is the form with yellow foliage. Both will grow to 4 ft and sow themselves regularly for years after the first planting. Giant red mountain orach is bigger and has bright crimson leaves and stems. It is a spinach and can be used for cooking as well as for the beauty of its leaves. The colour disappears when it is cooked.

For years I have used the milk thistle, *Silybum marianum*, to fill in odd spaces, for the leaves are most decorative with their white veinings and markings on grey-green. This is sometimes known as the Blessed Thistle, or the Holy Thistle, or Our

Lady's Milk Thistle, and it gets its name *marianum* from the legend that the white stains were caused by a drop of the virgin's milk falling on them. It eventually reaches 4 ft and produces many deep violet thistles. By this time the beauty of the leaves has gone, and I pull it out.

Grasses often strike a new note and the delicate shaking heads of quaking grass, *Briza minor* and *Briza maxima*, are pretty and take up little room. They are useful for cutting and can be used either fresh or dried. *Pennisetum caudatum** is a taller grass for growing in shade. *P. latifolium* has large nodding spikes, *P. c. ruppellii** is more bristling, but it is *P. villosum (longistylum)* that is most effective for lightening shade. It grows from 1 ½ to 2 ft high and has arching leaves and graceful flower stems ending in 6-in heads. They are twisted and covered with white or purplish down. These feathery plumes are delightful in the garden and are also very good for cutting.

Annual penstemon in lovely shades of pink, red and lavender grow to about 2 ft and are happy in shade, and so is the tall mallow, *Lavatera trimestris*, whether it is in white, pink or deep rose. The most beautiful, I think, is *L. t.* 'Loveliness', which grows to 2 ft only instead of 3 ft, and has flowers of the most sparkling shade of deep rose.

Orange is never an easy colour to place in the garden but it is easier in shade than sun, and in some dark places one can use the bright orange-scarlet of *Leonotis leonurus**, which delights in the colloquial name of Lion's Ear.

For places where something taller is needed there is *Leonurus sibiricus*, a labiate which has rosy pink flowers up a leafy stem. *Verbesina encelioides*, the Butter Daisy, has rather ragged-looking daisy flowers in glistening butter-yellow on 2-ft stems. The annual valerian, *Kentranthus macrosiphon**, with pink tubular flowers will grow in shade.

For a quick screen there is nothing like the annual hop, *Humulus japonicus* or it can as easily be grown to cover a bank. I have used the variegated form both as a trailing and climbing plant when I have wanted quick results in a shady position.

~ 10 ~

Personality Plants for Shade

Some of the most interesting plants that one can grow are shade lovers and I always feel sorry for people who have no shady corners in their gardens where they can grow the unusual and interesting plants that make a garden different.

Veratrums are quite common wild plants in Austria and other European countries but not so often seen in English gardens. One reason may be that they take some time to become reasonably sized plants if grown from seed and that is the best way to grow them. I believe they can also be increased by division, but I would not be brave enough to touch my plants and I think most people feel the same way. It is always the gardeners who do not possess a veratrum who want you to take off bits. I have ruined all sorts of plants by trying to accede to such importunity and now I am much more hard-hearted. And, anyway, even large and established plants of verartum grow slowly and make little additional growth each year.

The veratrum most often seen is *V. nigrum*, with tapering spikes of blackish purple flowers, which look like black velvet. The white variety, *V. album* has yellowish white flowers, and in *V. viride* the flowers are a soft grey-green. The individual blossoms that grow tight against the tall spires are delicately fashioned with veined petals and prominent stamens. The flower spikes rise from deeply-veined leaves which should be most attractive but always seem to be rather tattered at their pointed ends. I do not think it is always done by slugs and snails, although these creatures are partial to the flavour of veratrum; rough winds may be also to blame. I have seen veratrums grown in sun—there are handsome clumps in borders at Tintinhull and Newby Hall in Yorkshire, but it always seems to me that the woodland or informal garden is the place for them, and they should be grown as individual clumps or groups and not pushed in with a lot of other plants. I grow all three varieties in my ditch garden, they flower well and look at home rising from pockets made with big stones under the shade of trees.

It is surprising that *Kirengeshoma palmata* is still an unusual plant to many keen gardeners. It comes from Japan and has that distinction, and grace so often found in Japanese plants. One can tell just by looking at it that it needs to be grown in shade for it has the looks of a typical woodland plant, with its whippy black stems and soft green leaves which have been likened to those of the vine and the plane tree and are not quite like either. If I was asked to suggest what it resembles I would say the tulip tree, both for shape and texture. The flowers open in September, that is as far as they do open. They always look as if they could open much more, and I understand that there are forms which have more open flowers. Shuttlecocks is the definition often given to the flowers, which are soft, pale yellow, of crystalline texture and hover above the plant in airy flights. I grow it in a bed under a north wall in greensand, because it does not like lime, and must never be allowed to suffer from lack of moisture.

Not everyone appreciates the spiny beauty of *Fascicularia bicolor* but it has the fascination of the unusual. It will grow in sun but the best plants I know have always been in shade, and as it comes from Chile this is probably the best way to grow it. I have mine tucked into the bottom of a north wall near the angle made by a north-east wall. It needs some protection and should, I think, be grown against a wall or a boulder so that it opens out its slender spiny leaves to show its charms, like an anemone in a pool. Its light blue flower nestles at the base of the forest of leaves, and when flowering time is near the lower half of the leaves turn bright salmon-pink. Whether they blush from modesty or pride I do not know, but as the plant is usually pollinated by humming birds it is probably just another of nature's tricks. *Morina longifolia* is another plant with dangerous foliage. Its long prickly leaves are rather like those of a thistle, but they have a beauty of their own and when they are complemented with tall spikes of hooded white flowers the sight is memorable. The tubular flowers grow in whorls, nestling in prickly foliage, they turn from white to pink, and when they have been fertilised become crimson. I never cut down this plant for the skeleton stems have great beauty, and if one can bear to cut them make wonderful indoor decoration.

There is something very luxuriant and tropical about the ginger plants. They have large leaves somewhat reminiscent of a canna and long spikes of flowers which stand well above the foliage. In *Cautlea robusta** (*Roscoea cautleoides*) the leaves and stems have deep mahogany tints and the flowers are pale yellow. I grow this in a shaded, sheltered corner, and it flowers regularly and increases well. *Cautlea lutea** has deeper-yellow flowers and green leaves. I find the hedychiums do best in light shade such as is given by taller perennials or shrubs. They need a sheltered position and if they are given the full sun that is often recommended they do not survive a hard winter. I grow mine on the shady end of a south bank, and plant them so that they get protection from big stones. In a very hard winter the plants in the open have suffered but those protected by nearby shrubs came through quite happily. I have seen *H. densiflorum* peeping out from shrubs in gardens near London after really bad winters. *H. spicatum acuminatum** has big and handsome leaves and pale yellow flowers borne in a spike above the leaves. The flowers have protruding purple stamens and are scented. It needs a very sheltered position even in the south. *H. gardnerianum* is very similar and seems to possess the same measure of hardiness.

The hardy begonia, *B. evansiana**, is a colourful plant for a shady position. It grows about a foot high and the typical crinkled leaves grow at right angles so that one can see the markings on one side and crimson linings on the other. The pink flowers are small and grow in sprays above the leaves. When happy they even seed themselves. There is a white form with the same crimson stems and calyces. One of the joys of the countryside in summer is the white froth of cow parsley in the hedgerows. There is another parsley even more spectacular than Queen Anne's Lace, *Selinum carvifolia*, sometimes called Cambridge parsley because it is found in some Cambridgeshire fens. It is a lovely plant to grow under trees with its broad leaves more fern-like than any fern and large flat heads of white flowers. Red stems and black anthers are added charms to a magnificent plant that can grow to 5 to 6 ft, but is usually content at 4 ft. It grows well from seed, in fact the seedlings come up like mustard and cress. I grow this in the shade of my ditch and see that its soil is rich and never too dry.

The rhubarbs are handsome plants, and even the culinary variety could be grown for the beauty of its enormous leaves and great frothing spikes of flower. It is, in fact, sometimes grown this way, but the pink-flowered *Rheum palmatum* is even more colourful. Its enormous leaves are lined with red and when the 4-ft spikes of raspberry-pink flowers rise up above the leaves the effect is truly magnificent. It needs a moist position and I have been criticised for putting it at the top of a wall, with a north wall behind it, instead of growing it at the bottom of the ditch where the soil is really moist. I want to see the wonderful colours on the undersides of the leaves and the towering flower spike is much more spectacular when grown above the eye. I have another at the bottom of the ditch but I don't think it flowers as well. Perhaps the most exciting moment for this plant is when the first shoots appear. They are big rounded buds in shining cerise, more brilliant than the colour of a lobster's claw, and from them the crumpled red leaves gradually unfold.

A woodland plant that delights in shade and is very easy to grow is *Actaea spicata*, and yet one seldom sees it except in such gardens as Knightshayes in Devonshire and in Mr Norman Hadden's Porlock garden. It looks rather like a spiraea with small flowers until the flowers are over and then the spikes of large berries stand up well above the finely cut foliage. It can have black, white or red berries I used to think that the red-berried form, *A. rubra*, which I grow, was the most striking, but then I had not seen *A. alba* in fruit, and now I know that that is the loveliest of all. I caught a glimpse of it growing among shrubs in a shady garden

I was visiting and couldn't imagine—until I got near—what could be the lovely symphony of glistening white and feathery green.

Many gardeners grow phormiums in full sun but they do just as well in shade and it doesn't seem to make any difference to their flowering. I have several phormiums in the garden, those growing in the open perished in the winter of 1961–2 but all those growing under trees came through.

All the phormiums are beautiful with their broad stiff leaves 5 to 7 ft high and the magnificent plummy blue stems rising several feet above them. The flowers are rather a dull red, about 2 in long, on branching stems.

The ordinary *P. tenax* has smooth grey-green leaves with a darker edge. There are two variegated forms, *P. t. variegatum** is striped with creamy yellow and *P. t. veitchii**, which is more uncommon, has a broad golden stripe up the centre of each leaf. The purple phormium, *P. t. purpureum** has leaves with a crimson-purple sheen that glow like rubies in the late afternoon when the setting sun shines through them. There are at least four varieties of this phormium. The one most of us grow has leaves that are somewhat lax and bend backwards in rather an untidy way. There is a better form with leaves as stiff and straight as the green-leaved phormium. I have no name for a smaller edition of this phormium, which is about 3 ft high and the same rich colour, but the smallest of all, which grows to about a foot, is *P. t. alpinum**. Although I have had it for many years it has never flowered for me but it does increase slowly and is an attractive plant for the trough or rock garden. There is yet another phormium for the garden, *P. colensoi*, Mountain Flax, which has yellowish flowers and grows from 2 to 3 ft.

The New Zealand flax is not completely hardy, as many of us discovered in the cold winter of 1961–2, but it is hardier than many people think. I know an enormous clump, in a garden in the SW16 district of London, which survived the bad winter without even a shudder and flowered after it as well as it does every year.

Phormiums can be grown from seed or the sections can be taken off carefully one at a time, making sure that plenty of roots come too. It is a delicate operation which needs a sharp spade and a discerning eye.

Some of the symphytums make impressive clumps, worthy of standing alone in a shady corner. They are evergreen and when the flowering stems are cut off at the end of the season the large hairy leaves in a bluish shade of green make handsome rosettes.

*S. peregrinum** has light blue flowers after pink buds, on arching branched stems. It grows to 3 ft but increases slowly, which is not a bad idea when one thinks of the way some of the comfreys increase and seed themselves. *S. caucasicum* is one of the spreaders, but it is more dwarf, and has small rather greyish leaves. The flowers are deep gentian-blue. When I was given the white-flowered *S. tauricum** I was warned that it would spread and it does, by seeding profusely. The leaves are large and hairy and more green than some of the species. I get rather peeved when it comes up in all the places where I do not want it, but it has recently presented me with a magnificently variegated plant so I can be as brutal as I like. I have another variegated symphytum which I think is a variegated form of the common comfrey, *S. officinale*, with purple flowers on 3-ft stems. Another comfrey that was given to me and for which I have no name has deep crimson flowers. It is not a plant for a small garden, making a lot of foliage for very little flower, but it is right in a woodland setting.

Bocconia cordata is an old friend although everyone may not recognise it under its new name of *Macleaya cordata*. It is one of the loveliest foliage plants in the garden for its sturdy pink stems are clothed with shapely grey-green leaves lined with pearly grey. The clouds of tiny flowers in branching spires complete the picture, their colour is a soft buff and in *M. c.* 'Coral Plume'* have a pink tinge. It makes an imposing specimen plant but it needs a sharp spade to keep it in check if it increases too fast.

Judging by the number of people who ask me for its name *Thermopsis montana* is not grown very often and yet it is very easy to please. I grow it under the shade of an apple tree and enjoy its 3-ft stems with their grey-green leaves and greenish yellow flowers, which are not unlike a lupin but grow more gracefully. It spreads slowly by running roots but is not difficult to control.

Character is not governed by size and the foot-high Prophet Flower has something that takes it out of the ordinary. We have known it for ages as *Arnebia echioides** and it is hard to remember to call it *Macrotomia echioides*. A yellow borage is not at all common and this one has spots on each petal which look black but are really dark purple. They gradually dim and are practically gone by the time the flower begins to fade.

The variegated figwort, *Scrophularia aquatica**, grows well in shade and is evergreen, so that one enjoys rosettes of large leaves splashed and striped with cream all through the winter. I am always grateful when the time comes to cut off the top growth which gets rather tatty by the end of the summer. I remove the flowers the moment they open their little beady brown eyes but there is always the chance that one may want to take cuttings so the untidy top growth hangs on longer than is attractive. The name *aquatica*, I think, is correct although in so many lists this plant is given as *S. nodosa variegata*. I was given my plant—and name—by an eminent botanist and I stick to it. I have even looked for nodules on the roots when I have dug plants for friends and there are none, so *S. aquatica* it will remain.

There is a large and handsome spiraea that looks wonderful standing alone in a prominent place under trees. It used to be called *Spiraea aruncus* but now it has to be *Aruncus sylvester**. With its broad fern-like leaves and great plumes of cream blossoms it is a handsome sight especially if one catches glimpses of its magnificence before one actually comes upon it.

Silver plumes make pampas grass, cortaderia, a wonderful plant for late autumn and early winter but it must be used in the right way. Our Victorian forbears sickened many of us of this handsome plant by putting it in every garden, the smaller the better. It is not a thing you want just under your nose; it gets untidy after it has finished flowering and is much more effective when placed to show up against trees. It is a lovely sight at Sheffield Park in the autumn with the brilliant red of trees and shrubs and makes beautiful reflected pictures on the water. At Abbotswood in Gloucestershire it is most cleverly sited in broad landscape plantings, and at Abbotsbury in Dorset it makes an unusual hedge under trees.

I grow the dwarf pampas, *C. argentea pumila**, at the top of a flight of steps in my ditch garden. It is under an apple tree and makes a lovely picture from September till December. The normal pampas grass is about 7 ft and needs a wider landscape, and the best of this type is *C.* 'Sunningdale Silver', which has loose silky plumes 9 ft high. It is magnificent in a position where height is needed. The soft pink plumes of *C. a. carminea rendatleri** make a pleasant variation and it can be used in a very informal setting for its 10-ft plumes are slightly irregular against arching foliage. To get rid of the old leaves pampas grass should be set on fire each April. This is much better than cutting.

The giant thistle, *Cynara cardunculus*, has bold, silver-green leaves and is favoured by flower arrangers as well as gardeners.

Also late-flowering and attractive growing among shrubs the cimicifugas have great character and do best in shade in a cool and not-too-dry position. One should not be put off by the name of bugbane, which the plant gets because its peculiar smell is said to drive away bugs in Siberia, and no doubt other places. Its name is derived from the Latin *cimex*, a bug, and *filgo*, to flee, and an extract from the plant is used as an insecticide.

Some of the varieties do have a peculiar smell which may spoil them for some people but I have never noticed it. One, *C. simplex*, is probably the worst offender. It has arched branching stems of greenish yellow flowers and pale green foliage. It grows to about 3 ft and the best form is named *C. f. i.* 'White Pearl'. *C. americana* (*C. cordifolia*) is a little taller with pale green leaves rather like those of a maple and tapering spikes of cream flowers on naked stems. The foliage of *C. dahurica* is small and ferny and the flowers, which are tinged with blue, are in fluffy panicles on branching stems. The tallest is *C. racemosa*, which sometimes grows to 6 ft. This Japanese plant has curving pencil-thin flower spikes about 16 in long, on its slender stems.

The dianellas are Australasian lilaceous plants that need rather a sheltered position and are safe outside only in the southern half of England and elsewhere are more usually grown in a cold greenhouse. The most showy one is *D. tasmanica*, which has stiff leaves almost like a phormium and certainly wider than an iris and darker in colour. They are 3 ft high and make this a wonderful accent plant for a woodland position. The flower stalks are 4 ft with drooping bunches of pale blue flowers. But it is for the bright blue berries that come after that we grow this plant. *D. intermeda* is much smaller, with 15-in stems and white flowers, but again gives a very generous harvest of bright blue berries.

Another woodland plant grown for its berries chiefly is *Disporum oreganum**. It has cream flowers followed by very bright orange berries.

The fruits of podophyllum are nearly as exciting as the flowers. This too is a plant that delights in woodland conditions. Though a native of India it seems to be quite hardy here as I have seen it in gardens in different parts of the country. It always comes with a pleasant surprise when I see the smooth stems about 18 in high each topped by an elegantly divided leaf, which is often tinted with crimson. The flowers nestle in the middle of the leaves, and are white or pale pink. Later there are large shining red fruits, which are even more surprising. These fruits are edible but I do not think anyone would have the heart to eat such colourful ornaments.

Much of the personality of unusual plants is lost if they are grown very close to other flowers. Their leaves as well as their flowers are good, and the clumps look best grown singly with a background of shrubs or under the shade of trees.

~ 11 ~

A Shady Wall

Shady walls are not nearly so difficult as some people think. I have heard gardeners groaning about one north wall but in a shady garden there could be the equivalent of four north walls and they could all be attractively planted.

For anyone wanting to grow camellias shady walls are a godsend, for there is no place that suits them better, if the soil is right. This means soil that is cool, well drained and lime-free, a good mixture being two-fifths each soil and peat and one-fifth sand. In limy soils more peat is needed or a sequestrene can be used. In dry weather a mulch is a good idea. The japonica camellias are the hardiest and those with dark flowers show weather damage less than the white and pale pink types. The *williamsii* hybrids are good, particularly 'J. C. Williams', a clear shell-pink, which flowers for a long period, and 'Mary Christian', which is a deeper pink.

The climbing hydrangea, *H. petiolaris**, is a quick worker when it gets going, but it is sometimes rather slow to start. When it is covered with its large corymbs of creamy white flowers it is a wonderful sight. It does not keep its leaves but *H. integerrima** does, but is not very free flowering.

One should not be put off schizophragma by its dreadful name. It is not unlike the hydrangea, with one showy bract-like sepal to each cream flower. In *S. hydrangeoides* the bracts are deep cream, and paler in *S. integrifolia**.

The golden-flowered winter-flowering jasmine, *J. nudiflorum*, will grow anywhere and does not need the sun for it to open its golden flowers, which it does in late November and carries on for many months. It is very easy to please and every stem that can comes down and roots itself in the soil. The buds are flushed with brick-red and look lovely against the bright green stems. The leaves appear later and last throughout the year. The summer-flowering jasmine, *J. officinale* is another easy plant which delights in a shady wall. It produces its dark green foliage in moderation and starts flowering in June. I am usually cutting flowers in December, not very big ones but very sweetly scented. I was persuaded to buy *J. grandiflorum* which has larger, pink-flushed flowers, but found it made far too much foliage and there were not many flowers among the long sprays of greenery, so I cut it down, dug it up and gave it away.

Akebia quinata is practically evergreen, and being slender will grow up other plants on a north wall, or can be trained up the wall itself if it has something to twine on. Perhaps not very striking it is, nevertheless, an interesting plant with 5-

lobed leaves and dark chocolate-purple flowers which are scented. Male and female flowers grow on the same plant. Some years it produces large purplish violet fruits about 3 in long, which split open when ripe to show black seeds embedded in white downy pulp. It is a twining plant and hoists itself up on whatever is nearest, by its twining stems. It likes growing over a small tree or another plant, but makes use of wire-netting or whatever comes its way. The aristolochias have good foliage too, and grow rather in the same way as akebia. Their flowers are perhaps more curious than beautiful, being shaped rather like a Dutchman's pipe or siphon in shades of yellow-green and purple-brown. *A. macrophylla* is the form usually grown, *A. tomentosa* is rather smaller with a little down on the leaves. Mutisia does not make any pretence of doing without other plants. *M. retusa**, which has holly leaves and wide-rayed daisy flowers in a warm pink, comes from Chile and will climb to 8 ft if planted in moist soil on the north side of a shrub in a shady border.

Most garden books recommend that the everlasting pea, *Lathyrus latifolius*, should be grown on a sunny wall, but I grow it in shade and often see it on shady walls in cottage gardens. Normally it has purple-rose flowers, there is a good white form *L.* 'White Pearl'; *L.* 'Pink Beauty' is deep pink, and *L.* 'Red Pearl' rosy red. The brick-red *L. rotundifolius* is not quite hardy and needs a sheltered position, but a larger-flowered brick-red variety, which comes from Persia, grows on an east or north wall. *L. heterophyllus* has rather small flowers in a light red which are produced very freely. It makes a tangle of growth and does best if it can clamber on some other plant growing against the wall. It will sometimes seed itself in chinks in the wall and then it usually grows down instead of up.

One of the easiest plants for any wall position is, of course, virginia creeper, *Parthenocissus quinquefolia*, which is self-clinging and turns the most wonderful tints in autumn. But it does not do things by halves and is liable to take possession of any wall on which it finds itself. It can be reduced before it takes up too much space by cutting out whole stems. Ampelopsis, *P. trifoliata** (*Vitis inconstans*), is even more possessive but can be reduced if taken in time. We planted one on the highest wall of our house, which is shaded, but that did not restrain it so when it had covered the wall, an iron-barred window which could not be opened and was getting busy under the roof it had to be cut down, but it looked lovely against that old stone wall in young green, old green and brilliant autumn colour.

I wish the charming *P. henryana* had a quarter the exuberance of the other two. It needs to be grown in shade for the leaves to show that delicate network of white and purple variegation. In autumn they turn red. We all grow *Ampelopsis heterophylla** for its berries. I suppose it has flowers although I have never seen them, probably because I have never looked. But I always look anxiously to see if the plant will be hung with bunches of small, porcelain-blue 'grapes', which usually happens after a hot summer. The next year there are seedlings galore in the vicinity.

There are several good honeysuckles that do best on north walls. These are the woodland, large-flowered types which are liable to suffer from greenfly if grown in a hot position. *Lonicera tellmanniana** is very lovely, with rich yellow flowers, veined with red, but it is not scented. Both the early and late Dutch honeysuckles, *L. periclymenum belgica** and *L. p. serotina** are sweetly scented and flushed with purple on the outside of the flowers. They have particularly good dark red berries. *L. caprifolium* is scented with pink-budded creamy flowers and orange berries. *L. grata** is rather shrubby in growth with large sprays of scented pink and green flowers for several months. *L. japonica halliana** flowers a little later and is vigorous, both in flower and leaf. It flowers until frosts come and can be drastically reduced in spring, if needed.

Though all clematis like to be planted with their roots in shade (as in nature they grow among bushes) the large-flowered hybrids usually work through to the sun to flower. But there are quite a number of species that grow and flower well in shade. I have the Ludlow and Sherriff form of *C. orientalis** on a short west wall and of its own volition it goes round the corner on both sides to continue its triumphant progress on north walls. This is the orange-peel clematis, for the flowers have petals as thick as orange peel and though they start yellow they age to a soft orange colour. The foliage is very delicate and glaucous and it grows so luxuriantly for me that it covers everything in sight and has to be thinned in summer as well as being cut hard back in February. I have another on a shady east wall and have great trouble trying not to let it smother *C.* x *jouiniana* trained on the wall below it. *C.* x *jouiniana* is a semi-bushy clematis with exquisite Wedgwood blue flowers produced from August onwards. It grows well on a north wall or under trees and will cover unsightly objects or tree stumps.

C. tangutica is sometimes confused with *C. orientalis** as both have the same type of yellow lantern flowers and will grow in shade but *C. tangutica* flowers earlier than *C. orientalis**; the best form is *C. t.* Gravetye*, and it, like *C. orientalis** is covered in late autumn with large silky seed-heads like balls of down which last well into winter and are as picturesque as the seed-heads of 'old man's beard' which make our hedgerows so lovely in winter.

C. rehderiana grows on the same shady wall as *C. tangutica* and they have become entwined, so that there are bunches of small primrose-coloured flowers, which are scented of cowslips, growing with the yellow and silver of *C. tangutica*. The winter-flowering *C. calycina** (*balearica*) will grow and flower in shade. It has delightful evergreen ferny foliage in burnished dark green and small greenish ivory flowers freckled inside with maroon.

Though the white-flowered *Solanum jasminoides* needs a warm wall the more robust *Solanum crispum* will grow anywhere. The 'Glasnevin' form grows on a shady east wall and produces its mauve potato flowers with their golden centres for the whole summer and autumn.

A great deal has been written about Scotch creeper, alias the Flame Flower, alias *Tropaeolum speciosum* and it is always recommended that it should be planted on a north wall. That is one thing on which everyone agrees. After that it is supposed to work its way through to the sun to flower. But if the wall is very high or the tree on which it is growing goes up to heaven our friend will make the best of it and flower just as well in the shade. I have seen it flowering against a tall tree in complete shade and making its exciting blue berries, also on top of a hedge under trees and on a small shrub in a very dark shrub garden. *Berberidopsis corallina*, the Coral Plant of Chile, is a wonderful evergreen climber with dark leaves and hanging coral flowers, and that must be grown in shade.

There are more roses that will grow in shade than some people think. 'Mme Alfred Carrière', is the classic example, it grows and flowers prodigiously and to make an even more spectacular effect the shoots can be tied back instead of being cut off and so will produce even more flowers. 'Albéric Barbier' has scented double creamy white flowers and magnificent dark and glossy leaves and will easily reach 20 ft; 'Mermaid' is slow to start but will grow in sun or shade and is one of the loveliest with its large single yellow flowers and glossy foliage. It is not always long-lived when budded but small plants on their own roots are more likely to stay in the family a long time. The semi-double rosy scarlet 'Allen Chandler' is another vigorous rose for shade and I have seen the silvery pink 'Dr Van Fleet'* growing on a north wall. The various China roses, which are the garden roses of ancient China, grow in shade and bloom for most of the year. I have several on the north walls of my house, the old pink monthly rose, 'Fellemberg' in rose-crimson and a lovely silvery pink, which I think may be 'Hermosa', is planted next to a *Garrya elliptica* on a north wall and produces its flowers amid the grey-green leaves of the shrub. The green rose, *R. viridiflora**, which has crumpled green flowers and maroon centres, grows and flowers under a north hedge. *Rosa filipes* 'Kiftsgate', a climber from China, grows quite happily in shade and covers itself with flowers.

Ivies, of course, do not mind how shady it is. They can be those with delicate green leaves such as *Hedera helix feastii** and *sagittaefolia**, the dark green of Shield ivy, *H. h. deltoidea**, the parsley ivy, *H. h. cristata**, with its crisped leaves and bronze tones, 'Green Ripple', with pointed green leaves, and the frilled green 'Curly Locks'*. There are ivies with large leaves in green or variegated, such as *H. canariensis* and 'Gloire de Marengo', and tiny variegated ones in green and gold ('Jubilee') or silver ('Glacier' and 'Silver Queen'*).

Of all the shrubs to be trained against a shady wall the many varieties of

Cydonia (Japanese Quince) which now has to be called Chaenomales are among the toughest and longest lived, and they flower well and early. They can be grown as bushes or trained flat against the wall. In small spaces, such as under windows, the stems are grown horizontally if more convenient. The semi-double blood-red *C. x superba simonii** is low-growing naturally but can be trained on a wall. I grow white varieties in one or two dark corners, *C. japonica alba** will grow in the poorest soil, and *C. 'Snow'** is more open in habit. One of the most lovely for a low wall is *C. lagenaria moerloesii**, with the colouring of apple blossom.

Most of the escallonias are evergreen and I find that they do not mind a little shade. I grow the tall *E. iveyi** on a sunless east wall and *E.* 'Apple Blossom' in the shade of other shrubs. The white ones are not as a rule as tough as the coloured varieties but among the many good plants produced by Slieve Donard Nursery and bearing their name there is a hardy white. I grew the delicate arching *E. x edinensis** in a shady hedge, where it flowers well.

The tough pyracanthas, the firethorns, grow well in shade and there are many of them. I have had them on the east wall of my malthouse for very many years but like so many easy plants one is inclined to take them for granted, instead of being extremely grateful for their evergreen leaves, hawthorn flowers in June and brilliant berries in autumn. *P. coccinea lalandei** used to be grown very often, but now is superseded by *P.* 'Kanzan', which is finer in every way. Its berries are orange-scarlet, but in *P. atalantioides* (*P. gibbsii*) they are crimson-scarlet. *P. rogersiana* has rather orange berries, but in *P. r. flava** (*P. fructo-luteo**) and *P. angustifolia* the berries are yellow.

Cotoneasters, of course, are not all evergreen, but those that are not usually make such a filigree of stems that they are interesting all the time. *C. horizontalis*, for instance has leaves that turn brilliant crimson before they drop, the white flowers become red berries which adorn the herring-bone stems for several weeks. I used *C. lactea** to cover an ugly north wall made of stucco on a kitchen extension and nothing could be more satisfactory than its curtain of grey-green leaves and the berries which ripen in winter are almost as bright as holly and remain much longer. *C. franchetii* is evergreen too and makes a graceful bush or small tree growing against or over a shady wall.

Among the trees and shrubs for a shady wall I would put *Forsythia suspensa* high on the list, if one lives in an area where birds leave the buds to open into flowers. I have had the pale-flowered *F. s. pallida** against the east wall of my malthouse for many years, it flowers extremely well and we prune it hard after flowering. Laburnums, rosemaries and deutzias all do well in shade and so does *Viburnum tomentosum plicatum grandiflorum**, which is a sturdy spreading bush, with dark, deeply veined leaves, which turn crimson in autumn, and creamy white snowball flowers spaced evenly along the branches. *Berberis stenophylla* makes a large graceful bush and can be pruned hard after flowering. It has small dark leaves and apricot flowers for a month in spring.

When *Garrya elliptica* is mentioned one always thinks of the plant with its long and graceful catkins in palest green. It is a lovely shrub and looks best on a north wall, but the lady of the species is beautiful too and has tight clusters of fruits which turn from green to rich-bloomed purple.

Fatsia japonica (*Aralia japonica*) is a magnificent foliage shrub for shady places. The leaves are almost a foot across, dark, shiny and fingered, with large heads of white flowers in autumn, which last into the winter. It does not mind how deep the shade and will grow to 15 ft on a sunless wall. *Fatshedera* x *lizei** is another shrub for shade, a cross between fatsia and ivy, and has smaller, very glossy leaves which are beautiful at all times. Its flowers are bronze and look like the ivy side of its parentage. It will grow well against a shady wall and soon makes a wide bush. The variegated form is not so free-growing but is pretty grown from the top of a shady wall.

I have an affection for the very ordinary *Mahonia aquifolium* when it stays in the wall in which I found it, but do not love it so much when it comes out into the bed where I grow hellebores. It will grow anywhere in shade and its glossy leaves are always good. When there is nothing else to pick in early spring the bright crimson of its young growth is as good as a flower. When *Mahonia japonica* has finished flowering *M. aquifolium* starts, its yellow flowers are not scented but they are followed by fruit as blue and bloomed as a grape and which give it its name of oregon grape.

Osmanthus delavayi flowers so early in the year that sometimes its white flowers—tubular and sweetly scented—are spoilt by frost. It is evergreen, with small dark leaves, and it dislikes hot sun so is a good shrub for a shady spot.

If *Kerria japonica* was a difficult shrub we should think a lot more of it. But as it is easy and will grow anywhere (it is the Jews' mallow of cottage gardens) we take it very much for granted. Fresh green stems, bright young shoots and flowers which are either yellow and single or orange and double spangle the branches. It is happy in shade and flowers for a long time.

For a narrow bed under a north wall where something rather small and choice is needed the sarcococcas might be chosen. They are attractive in their small way and can easily be overlooked in big plantings. They are members of the box family and are good under the north wall of a courtyard or some place equally intimate where their scented flowers in January would be noticed and enjoyed. I have never had bushes big enough to cut, but I can imagine their glossy evergreen leaves with the creamy flowers—mostly tufts of stamens and stigmas—would be delightful in the house. In *S. confusa*, *S. humilis** and *S. ruscifolia* the flowers are creamy white and the black berries are often on the bushes at the same time, and in *S. hookeriana digyna* the flowers are pink-tinted and turn to red berries.

There are plants that will grow in a shady wall as well as on it or against it. Small ferns, saxifrages, house leeks and many of the small shade-loving rock plants can be introduced as small plants into welcoming chinks and will grow and seed themselves. Some of the small plants growing at the base of the wall will reach up, *Erigeron mucronatus** does, and, of course, the periwinkles do. The yellow *Corydalis lutea* seeds itself in any old shady wall and I find seedlings of *Erinus* 'Dr Hanele'* from plants growing on top of the wall on the north side just as often as in the sun.

~ 12 ~

Gold and Silver

Although as a general rule plants with golden leaves prefer to be in sun, there are several that have to be grown in shade, and though one can take it that a sunny garden is the best place for the many plants with silver foliage, owners of shady gardens are not debarred from all the helpful silver plants.

The form of *Lamium maculatum* with golden leaves has not the stamina and determination of the ordinary green-leaved lamiums. I had great difficulty in keeping it until I grew it in shade. Now I put in small pieces in a narrow shady border at the bottom of a wall and each piece increases and soon makes a good clump. Another place where it does well is at the top of the ditch bank under the shade of a hedge.

It is strange that Mr Bowles' golden grass, *Milium effusum aureum**, has to be grown in shade but this is certainly where it does best and seedlings come up in very shady places. It is a golden form of a British native grass, which has leaves, stems and flowers all the same shade of bright gamboge yellow. It grows 12 to 18 in high in most gardens, although I have seen it taller, and is a wonderful plant to bring a patch of gold to a dark corner. There is no mistaking the seedlings, they are brilliant gold when less than an inch high and it is very easy to rescue them from places where they'll be hidden and assemble them in a colony.

The golden veronica, *Veronica teucrium trehane**, is a difficult plant to keep but I think it will stay in the family if it is given the shade of a taller perennial or shrub. I grow the golden marjoram, *Origanum vulgare aureum**, in shady places and it seems to be as golden as when grown in sun. The curled form is tougher than that with small uncurled leaves, which is more difficult to keep and far better in shade.

As a rule plants with golden shiny leaves do best in sun but both the golden-variegated forms of elaeagnus do well in shade. The one most usually grown is *E. pungens aureo-variegata** and that will grow anywhere. Its leaves are mostly rich gold and have a narrow green margin. Although it will give radiant colour all through the winter in an open position it will do just as well on a sunless wall and is an excellent plant to bring sunshine to dark corners. The other, slower-growing variety, *E. pungens dicksonii**, has the colouring reversed with a narrow green stripe down the middle of each golden leaf, and this has to grow in shade. The golden privet, *Ligustrum ovalifolium aureum**, will grow quite well in shade, and I have it on one or two east walls.

There are two golden-leaved subjects that I have nearly lost by planting them in sun. The golden form of the Cornish elm makes a delightful upright tree which grows very slowly and I thought it would be just the thing for one of my terraced beds. But I was the only one who thought so. The poor thing showed its distress very clearly; it looked so unhappy that visitors thought its poor condition was due to chlorosis, I thought it was my soil, and it was some time before I realised that all it wanted was the comfort of shade.

I thought I should please the gold philadelphus, *P. coronarius aureus**, by putting it in sun, but this again was wrong. The leaves have a sensitive matt surface and do far better in shade. This is one of the golden-leaved plants that turns greenish yellow in mid-summer.

The recognised position for the silver-foliaged plant is in poor soil in a hot dry position, but many of them will grow in shade if the soil is dry and poor. By accident a seedling of *Senecio* 'White Diamond' was planted in a shady bed and to my surprise it has increased well and is as startlingly white as any I have planted in sun.

The silver santolinas grow well in shade too, I have an enormous bush of *Santolina neapolitana** in the shady corner made by a north and east wall, and it is as white as any other in the garden. The neat *S. incana** also grows well in shade.

The artemisias are not so insistent on sun as some silvers, *A. stelleriana* has almost white chrysanthemum-shaped leaves on its prostrate stems and shade happens to have reached the place where it grows without changing its appearance. I planted some spare *A. ludoviciana* in a shady bed and it keeps its white appearance and so does *A. absinthium* and the improved form *A. a.* 'Lambrook Silver'. *A. lanata** grows near some small conifers and is sometimes patchy, but where it can get under the shade of the tree it remains white and silky and altogether far more luxuriant.

Some of the helichrysums do not seem to mind a little shade. The narrow-leaved *H. angustifolium** with its golden flowers and curry smell has made an enormous bush in shade and although most of my plants of the other, broader leaved curry plant, *H. serotinum** (*siculum**), grow in sun, I have one that is in rather a shady corner. The small bush *H. trilineatum** is also happy in shade.

Anaphalis triplinervis grows just as well in shade and so does the taller *A. margaritacea*, so I expect the very tall *A. m. yedoensis** will too. Even the tough *Senecio greyi** will grow under trees if the soil is poor and dry.

~ 13 ~
Bergenias

It is a brave woman who embarks on the subject of bergenias (megaseas is the name they used to have), because it is a big and complicated family and some of the varieties are very similar, and although several eminent botanists are working on the subject not many of their findings have been published so far.

Looking through a dozen catalogues from well-known nurseries I find great variation in the names of the species, some I have never heard of before, others are fancy or descriptive names, designed to give a picture of the plant but which tell nothing of its origins.

I cannot leave bergenias out of this book as they are eminently good plants for a shady garden. The Victorians had a great deal of shade in their gardens and they grew a large number of bergenias, although they did not call them that. In those days the plant was still *Saxifraga megasea* or the elephant-leaved saxifrage and it was just left at that without any qualifying variety. In his *English Garden* William Robinson simply refers to *S. ciliata* and *cordifolia**.

Most people have now become very bergenia-minded, but there are still some who class them with privet and ferns, pampas grass and monkey puzzle trees, and other Victorian garden features. But I think even this minority will come to appreciate the beauty and diversity of the many-purpose bergenia.

To enumerate their good qualities I will start with their good temper and adaptability. They do not mind at all where they grow, in sun or shade, in soil with or without lime, in walls or paving, fat living in rich beds or starvation in poor soil. You can pull bits off at any time and each piece will grow without the leaves showing any sign that an operation has taken place, in fact I cannot remember ever seeing a wilting bergenia. Sometimes a chunk of the massive stem is left from the operation and though it has no root and no leaf it will still grow if it is planted in sandy compost.

Their second good point is the colour they give in winter. The forms with the very big leaves turn brilliant scarlet and remain so for months on end. The rather narrower-leaved varieties, such as *B. delavayi** and *B. beesiana** (which some people say are the same but not in my garden) are lined with crimson and when in winter the top of the leaves turn plum-purple the effect is really sumptuous.

The flowers of bergenias I would put last on the list. They are delightful and very pleasant to have so early in the year but I regard them as a dividend on which one cannot count. For they do not always flower, at least not for me, and I do not think anyone knows how to make them. For many years I have had a rather rare white-flowered plant called *B. milesii**. I assume it is white-flowered but as it has never flowered for me I have no means of knowing. Another very small one has lived with me for nearly twenty years. I have given pieces to many people and their plants flower the first year, yet I have never had the suspicion of a flower. It cannot be because they resent interference otherwise the bits I chisel off and stick in someone else's wall would not flower at once. I have read that bergenias will grow well in shade and that they need a certain amount of sun to flower well, but I do not think there is any truth in this. Some of the finest flowers I have had have been in the shadiest parts of the garden. I have tried potash, and old farmyard manure, bonemeal and copious watering, but cannot say that any of these remedies had recognisable effect on the flowering of plants. Probably the weather has most to do with it, and that is something we cannot control. Bergenias do well in town gardens like most plants with shiny leaves, and they are just the sort of plant to use to give a colourful furnished look at all times of the year.

Probably the commonest bergenia is *B. cordifolia*, with large heart-shaped leaves. This varies considerably but the commonest form has large trusses of deep pink flowers held on thick stems above the leaves. The form attributed to Miss Jekyll—and it is understood she liked *B. cordifolia* best of all the bergenias—has particularly large leaves and enormous heads of deep pink, almost magenta, flowers, standing high above the leaves on sturdy red stems, 12 to 18 in high. The experts seem to agree that Miss Jekyll's *cordifolia* and *cordifolia purpurea* (from Siberia) are the same. There was once a form of *B. cordifolia* with leaves variegated with gold and we should all like to find it again. I do not believe it is known to be in existence today although one always hopes to find it in some forgotten garden. That, I fear, is not very likely as forgotten gardens are always getting scarcer and with so many people seeking out the rare plants it is not likely that a variegated treasure—most popular of all—would be overlooked. My hope is that one of my plants will suddenly develop variegation. It happens with symphytums, primroses, geraniums and dandelions, among others so why not bergenias?

I have a very neat bergenia with short-stemmed rounded leaves and pale pink flowers, which have conspicuous green stamens. It is a good plant to grow among stones as it nestles down among them with great complacency. Its leaves are a very bright fresh green and do not colour much. The local nursery always refer to it as Lambrook Pink and I think I shall give it that name to distinguish it. My unnamed miniature also has rounded leaves with short stems and is considered by experts to be a form of *cordifolia*. I believe there is also a white *cordifolia*, but I have not seen it.

B. crassifolia is nearly as common as *B. cordifolia*. It is very easy to please and increases very quickly. There is no mistaking its identity because its large oval leaves turn back from the stalk and round the edges so that they are like the rounded shape of the back of a spoon. In colour they are rather a light green and have a very shiny surface, not nearly so tough-looking as *B. cordifolia*. This is the bergenia the late E. A. Bowles called Pigsqueak because the leaves when pulled through the fingers made a squeaking sound. It comes from Central Asia and is one of the easiest to flower with rather pale pink, faintly scented flowers, which sometimes open as early as January. There are several different forms, *B. c. orbicularis** is one and *B. c. ovata* has slightly narrower leaves.

The bergenia that flowers best with me is the one that has recently been identified as *B.* x *schmidtii* ('Crassifolia' x 'Ligulata'), and I think is the least attractive of all the bergenias but the most co-operative to increase and flower. It has rounded, rather spoon-shaped leaves on long stems and is the one often seen in cottage gardens and growing in cottage walls. My first plant was given to me by a friendly baker's roundsman before the war. He had a garden full of it and called it 'winter heliotrope' and asked if I would like some. I had no idea what I was getting and that it was to be my introduction to bergenias, for which I have always been grateful.

There are several bergenias with slightly narrower leaves which are particularly brilliant in the winter. The leaves are lined with crimson and as they are held upright, like a terrier's ears, and the other sides of the leaves take on rich tones of purplish crimson in the winter they are well worth growing. I like to grow them on a raised bed so that on a sunny day the light shines through them and they glow like rubies. They all have rather deep pink flowers early in the year. *B. purpurascens* has the darkest flowers and rather neat, well-coloured leaves. Both *B. delavayi** and particularly *B. beesiana** have brilliantly coloured leaves lined with crimson. These bergenias are not so good for ground cover as the commoner varieties, they do not increase very quickly and with their upright growth have no spreading habit.

The next roughly bracketed group are not completely hardy, and after a bad winter it is not unusual to see the pink-flushed white flowers in their crimson calyces on bare stems. The leaves are large and slightly hairy at the edges like a dog's ears. *B. stracheyi* is the hardiest and produces its light mauvish pink flowers in March. *B. ligulata** has the same hairy leaves and is not completely hardy. It has white flowers shaded pink with handsome crimson anthers. *B. rubra* and *B. speciosa* are considered to be variations of *B. ligulata**. With me *B. ciliata* is the most active of these types, it has creeping stems and increases very well and though it sometimes takes a beating in a hard winter it soon recovers. Its flowers are large and flesh-coloured with conspicuous red calyces and are later than some. *B.*

*stracheyi milesii** is slow to increase and reluctant to produce its white flowers, but it is one of these tantalising plants that keep one hoping.

There are many variations of all the species and many are given names which may not be valid. Some come with wonderful descriptions and do not live up to them. I was given one that I was assured had blue flowers. The owner thought most highly of this bergenia and was loth to part with it. Luckily he was anxious to acquire Mr Bowles' special rhubarb so we were able to make an exchange that pleased us both. I shared my spoils with other enthusiasts and we all waited eagerly for it to flower. When it did flower in the Oxford Botanic Garden (it has not flowered for me yet) the flowers were the usual sad pink, and I have often wondered if a different soil had produced blue flowers or if its colours appear different to some people. Another I was given was said to be exceptionally tall in growth, but so far I have not noticed a bergenia on stilts in my garden.

The most striking of all the hybrids, of course, is 'Ballawley Hybrid'* from Dublin. I had heard varying theories about this so I made enquiries from the Slieve Donard Nursery in Northern Ireland who now handle it. It is sometimes called Delbees and sometimes Ballawley and now I know that when Mr Shaw-Smith of the now extinct Ballawley Nursery near Dublin raised the plant he talked about the name Delbees as being suitable because it suggested the parentage—*delavayi** x *beesiana**. When Mr Smith gave up the nursery the Slieve Donard Nursery acquired the complete stock and though for a while they used the name Delbees they did not like it and when they exhibited it in London they changed the name to Ballawley Hybrid with Mr Smith's permission. This explanation disposes of one theory—that the parents are *B. delavayi** and *B. cordifolia*.

B. 'Ballawley Hybrid'* is a wonderful plant, with the biggest leaves of any bergenia. They are a very good, fresh green for most of the year and more glossy than any other bergenia. At the approach of winter they turn a really brilliant plum-crimson and they remain like that until warmer weather returns and then overnight they are green again. It is then that the flowers appear, large magenta-pink on graceful drooping heads on thick red stems. To keep this magnificence unharmed by winter winds the plant needs a sheltered position. Though the leaves are large they are not tough and leathery and rough weather crumples and tatters them, even tears them off altogether, which is a tragedy as they give us brilliant colour for several months. It definitely does best in shade.

There are three interesting German introductions, *B.* 'Abendglut', which has dark rose-crimson flowers, *B.* 'Morgenröte', which is bright rose-pink and flowers in August and September, and *B.* 'Silberlicht', which I think is the loveliest of the three, with pink-flushed buds opening to white flowers. Some nurseries list these under their English renderings of 'Evening Glow', 'Day Blush' and 'Silver Light'.

B. 'Sunshade' is so named because of its rounded sprays of rosy pink flowers rising from large oval reddish bronze leaves. 'Croesus' is a very dwarf hybrid between *B. cordifolia* and *B. purpurascens* with richly coloured foliage and deep pink flowers. *B.* 'Bee's Pink' is also dwarf, with good pink flowers.

Mr H. C. Pugsley of Derby has made several very successful crosses, one of the best being between *B. beesiana** and *B. purpurascens*, which combines the best of both parents in brilliantly coloured leaves and deep-toned flowers.

Many of us are making collections of bergenias and the question arises on how to house so many rather large plants. I like to grow mine between stones, either at the edge of a bed or a path, or on bank, and I have many of them in my ditch garden. They look particularly well at the edge of paving and will even grow in a wall, although I would not risk this with my more precious varieties unless I had quite a number of plants.

~ 14 ~

Euphorbias

At first glance it might seem that euphorbias are more sun-loving than plants for shade, but this is not so. I grow a large number of euphorbias and nearly all of them in shade, and I know many shady gardens where they grow equally well. The two sun lovers, *E. myrsinites* and *E. biglandulosa**, probably do better with a stone behind them in a hot dry place, but even they will grow and flower in shade that is not too dense.

Euphorbias have become very fashionable of recent years, for we have discovered the value of their magnificent foliage, which is beautiful on every day in the year. The one that most people buy first is *E. wulfenii**, I know I did. It was my introduction to euphorbias and I lived with it for several years without knowing a great deal about it or the possibilities of the genus. I used to wonder why it did not flower every year, but even that did not worry me much as I bought it primarily for its foliage.

I still do not know why some euphorbias do not flower regularly every year; I have one big one that has never flowered, I wish I did know because I am often asked. As soon as they get into a good rhythm it is usually satisfactory, one cuts off the stems which have produced flowers and new ones come up to take their place. Sometimes a surgical operation is beneficial. My very big plant growing in stones on the terrace had to receive surgical treatment for the centre was congested with all the stumps of the stems that had been cut down over the years. When cutting them out some of its stomach came too and we had to tie up the patient and support it round the outside to stop it from falling apart and opening up the wound. But instead of becoming an interesting invalid it was soon exuberant with health and we had 225 flower-heads on it that year. In honesty I must own up that that was its last really good fling, it went back afterwards and has now had to be replaced, but I think it shows that cutting out the dead wood is a good idea, but probably a little each year rather than a very drastic clearance after several years.

There are three large euphorbias very much alike, and some of the plants sold as *E. wulfenii* may be *E. sibthorpii**, which has dark brown, almost black eyes, and *E. characias**, which is usually smaller and neater and has really black eyes. The one I had as *wulfenii* was, I now think, *E. sibthorpii**, for the real *wulfenii* has orange eyes. It is the biggest of the three and the best specimen I have seen was in the garden of the late Walter Butt at West Porlock. Another very big one I remember was under a tall yew tree at the bottom of some steps in one of the many big gardens I have visited. I have forgotten the name of the garden but I shall never forget the colour contrast of the very dark tree and the blue-green spurge in its shade. At Dartington Hall the euphorbias are growing in a wall above which large gorse plants are planted and that colour scheme is very happy too.

The real *E. wulfenii** gets very big sometimes and if packed in a corner does not always know what to do with its arms and legs. I grew one from a cutting from Walter Butt's Porlock plant and put it in a corner made by two walls, and now that it has grown it is far too crowded. It really needs enough room to become a large symmetrical bush, in a wide border, as under the high wall at Tintinhull where it manages to grow without being cramped, and is lovely among other shrubs and roses, and seeds itself regularly.

*E. characias** makes a smaller, neater bush, and its flower-heads are neater too. They always remind me of busbies in shape. It is black-eyed and seems to flower regularly each year. I have it in several shady places in the garden and find it flowers and seeds extremely well. It is the euphorbia that the late E. A. Bowles grew in his shady garden and which he mentions in one of his books. Some visitors going round the garden saw the plant and asked a garden lad who was working nearby what it was. He replied: 'I do not rightly know, but we boys calls it the frog spawn bush.' Nothing could be more apt and the name has stuck. There is a variation of the plant which has little green tufts among the flowers (usually called *vivepara*) which make wonderful cuttings and would no doubt root if the stems were bent down so that the flower-heads touched the ground. The flowers of this particular form are rather looser in growth and paler in colour.

There are two very big euphorbias which can be used to fill any shady corner. I grow them both in a bed made by angles of north and east walls. *E. androsaemifolia** has a solid fleshy root and makes long stems with heads of smallish flowers. After the flowers are over the stems are cut down and a forest of new and fresh green shoots cover the clumps. This euphorbia can be increased by seed or by division of the root. *E. valde-villoscarpa** is one of the biggest I know, with very long thick stems covered with darkish foliage and typical ephorbia flowers.

In this shaded comer I also grow *E. sikkimensis* and *E. griffithii*. We used to think *E. sikkimensis* most colourful before *E. griffithii* was introduced, and it still is, particularly when the new growth in brilliant coral comes through the ground. Later the foliage becomes more green but the plant is still a wonderful sight when it is a mass of love-bird-green bracts. They glow even in a dark corner. In Mr Hadden's Porlock garden this euphorbia grows magnificently under trees, it spreads in all directions with its underground roots, which come up as bright coral shoots and then produce leaves of blue-green edged and veined with brilliant red.

E. griffithii runs too and I wish it would run more because each shoot can be severed to make a new plant. Its glory is in fiery orange bracts which glow like living embers for many weeks. Not all the plants raised from seed are good and the best results are obtained from cuttings which sometimes take a long time to root. The best form of *E. griffithii* has now been named, and very well named, *E. g.* 'Fireglow', and anyone buying this will have the best form available. I like to grow this plant among other substantial subjects. It is not the right kind of plant to stake and yet its 3- to 4-ft stems get blown about in the late autumn when the foliage is turning to gold and crimson.

It is always recommended that *E. palustris* should be grown in a moist spot. This may apply if it is planted in sun, but grown in shade as I grow it, it does quite well in an ordinary bed. It needs plenty of room for its long and well-furnished stems and handsome greeny gold flowers.

E. mellifera, the honey spurge, is said to need moisture too, as well as some protection. I grow it in a narrow bed under a north wall as well as in a fairly exposed part of the garden and it comes through the worst winters, although sometimes cut to the ground. It makes an impressive bush about 4 ft high and has small honey-scented flowers, with rather unusual angular fruits.

The densely green *E. robbiae** is adaptable and fits into many awkward spaces next to buildings, or under trees, and is used in this way in the gardens of Magdalen College, Oxford, and in the Oxford Botanic Garden. I first saw it under a hedge in a small garden made on a Devonshire hillside. There was a big tree nearby taking much of the nourishment from the soil but the euphorbia had worked its way along in the shade to fill the space between hedge and path with dark green handsome evergreen foliage and heads of bright green flowers. It is shorter and fleshier than some euphorbias and its flowers last the whole year, the new buds forming in December before one has had time to cut off last year's flowers. One of the places in which I grow it and in which it is very happy is at the base of willows which hold up a bank in the ditch.

E. amygdaloides is definitely a woodland plant but a very handsome one with reddish seems and rather a bushy habit. The best form is *E. a. superba** with bigger and better everything. It is almost more famous for its variations than for itself. I think the only variegated perennial euphorbia being grown today is *E. a. variegata**. This wonderful plant is best seen where it originated in Mr Walpole's famous garden, Mount Usher, near Dublin. There it is at its beautiful best, in the embrasures of a wall. It needs regular propagation otherwise it can disappear in the night or go back to plain green. Luckily this is one of the euphorbias that grow easily from cuttings when one has learnt the trick of sealing the cut stalk with a lighted match. I have no name for the other colourful variation of

E. amygdaloides and for my own convenience I call it *E. a. rubra**, because of its reddish leaves, which are quite different from any other spurge I know. It was given me from Ireland and I am glad it makes a few seedlings so that I am sure of keeping it. It is much more dwarf than the other forms of the woodland spurge, and with me has never made a big plant.

There seem to be two forms of *E. hyberna*, the Irish spurge, for the one that grows wild in some parts of Ireland and Somerset is not the same as the form one sees in botanic gardens. The wild one is a rather woody plant that clothes the banks of a valley on Exmoor. It has strong and heavy roots and the piece I was offered, from the garden of a friend who lives in the valley, was not the easily dug little seedling it appeared. Not to be beaten my cousin's chauffeur who had driven us managed to extricate the small plant with a gear lever. I still have that piece and it is not much bigger after half a dozen years. It does not ramble or seed but it can be relied on to make a large and colourful clump under trees of bright green-gold on foot-high stems, which remains dazzling for several weeks.

The other form of *E. hyberna* is a lighter, more fragile-looking plant. It has fresh green leaves and big heads of yellow-green flowers, rather small in themselves but effective in a mass. It seeds itself very generously and it is impossible not to recognise the seedlings at once, with their almost translucent green leaves, which have darker markings.

The best euphorbias for the border are the March-flowering types which make rounded hummocks of gold early in the year. *E. epithymoides** is a neat and colourful plant in May when it dazzles all admirers, but it gets out of hand later and should be trimmed after flowering, something I do not do as drastically as I should as I have never yet mastered the art of making its stubborn cuttings root and must have material for another try.

There has been some confusion but I think it is now agreed that *E. epithymoides** and *E. polychroma* are synonymous. *E. pilosa* and *E. p. major** are very similar to *E. epithymoides** but flower later and are not so rounded and neat in their clumps. But they flower again on their 18-in stems in the autumn and the foliage takes on beautiful shades of pink and lavender to enhance the display. The cuttings of *E. pilosa* are not any easier to strike than those of *E. epithymoides**.

A controlled border is no place to introduce Ploughman's Mignonette, that busy little runner *E. cyparissias*. But this is a lovely plant in the right place, and that, I think, is as ground cover under trees. I grow it under a large *Cupressus arizonica* and it does very well. It is a dwarf plant with ruffled green stems seldom more than 9 in and bright gold flowers.

The best spurge for autumn colour is undoubtedly *E. dulcis*, a rather slight little plant with small rounded leaves all the way up its stems. It is the leaves that turn such wonderful shades of crimson and gold in late summer and autumn; the flowers are rather small and not particularly outstanding. This plant colours as well in shade as in sun and I notice that many of its seedlings come up in quite shady places. *E. corallioides* is a much taller plant, but with the same small rounded leaves, which do colour but not so gorgeously. It grows to about 3 ft with a wide branching head. I grow it between a stone trough and a wall, with a weeping silver pyrus above, *Acanthus mollis* in front and the pink- and cream-variegated *Polygonum cuspidatum** behind, and the effect is very good.

E. capitata is a miniature and a running one at that, but it does not run very far or very fast. It has particularly blue glaucous foliage and little yellow-green flowers. In *E. corollata* there is a white collar beneath the flower. This smallish upright plant is a treasure for a shady bank.

Another small spurge is the pretty little one that grows on Portland. I noticed it in miniature arrangements when I was judging floral exhibits and of course had to find out all about it. I made a pilgrimage to Portland and collected seed and am quite certain I shall have *E. portlandica* for the rest of my life. It makes neat little bushy plants about 6 in high in very blue glaucous foliage and keeps its children close at hand. Another sea spurge grows on the Gower Peninsula and parts of Ireland and England. *E. paralias* is a taller, more robust plant than *E. portlandica*, with fleshy stems about a foot high, very glaucous, with thick overlapping leaves. It is a perennial and is best propagated by seed.

Most people know the biennial caper spurge, *E. lathyrus*, and many of us both love and hate it. It is one of the best foliage plants in the garden, and beautiful at every moment of its life, but we have too much of it. I would hate to be without a few of its handsome upright plants in the garden, but I do not want a thousand. The Tintern spurge, *E. stricta*, is an annual and a very attractive one. It makes a cloud of very small very bright green leaves and has red stems. One of its seedlings came up in front of a large plant of *E. characias**, and the contrast of golden-green against the stern blue-green was lovely for the whole summer.

The other annual spurge, *E. marginata*, is not at all obliging in the matter of seedlings. The seed has to be collected, sown and carefully reared, but it is worth the trouble to have the white-veined and margined leaves, with their white bracts and soft green leaves. It comes from the southern States of America and is known as Snow on the Mountain, and is sometimes used for buttonholes. It does not like such dense shade as most of the euphorbias but it will tolerate a little.

~ 15 ~

Hellebores

No plants are better suited to the shady garden than hellebores, for they need a shady site and are wonderful plants for growing under deciduous shrubs and trees or under north walls. Being evergreen except in the case of *H. viridis*, *H. intermedius**, *H. purpurascens**, *H. dumetorum**, *H. atrorubens**, and *H. cyclophyllus**, they furnish the garden throughout the year with their great fingered leaves in dark green. They usually seed very freely and there is always the excitement of seeing what the new plants will be. For they do not always seed true and I fear they are rather promiscuous plants, but they are all beautiful. All the same I wish the rare 'Black Knight' and 'Ballard's Black' would seed true, for these are among the most exciting of the hellebores and so often their seedlings are a medium pink instead of a purple that should be dark as night.

Hellebores can be increased by division, of course, and this is the only way to be sure you are getting the exact plant. There is scarcely a moment when this operation cannot be performed, and every scrap will grow shoots, bits of crown without buds or bits of stalk with a scrap of root adhering—but of course it takes time, and there is a limit to the number of divisions that can be made, however small they are.

If possible I think hellebores should be grown as separate clumps so that each plant makes a picture with flowers and leaves; in this way one keeps the colours distinct and there is a chance that the seedlings will be more or less true. It always seems wasteful when these plants are allowed to make large drifts of assorted colours, although I admit that my way of taking the children from the parents and growing them on separately does take a certain amount of time.

I like to come across my hellebores in odd places, and I have favourite positions for all of them, but as I add more and more to my collection the supply of shady places is running out. I try to get as many as I can at the top of banks and on raised beds so that it is possible to look up at the flowers. This is particularly important in the case of the *guttatus** hybrids, which are heavily stippled inside the flowers, and all be very exciting.

I am not alone in finding *H. niger* the most difficult of all the hellebores to please, and this is one that I do leave alone, and always refuse to lift and divide my plants. The irony of it is that the people who do not take any trouble always have the best Christmas Roses, and those of us who fuss and cosset our plants get very poor results. And we are always looking for the perfect variety, with very early, very big flowers which have nice long stalks. I like mine to have a pink flush on the outside of the flowers although there are many who consider the pure white forms are the most beautiful. *H.* 'Potter's Wheel' comes in this category, and it has enormous flowers on long stalks so I do not wonder that at the moment the demand far exceeds the supply. I never refuse the offer of a Christmas Rose because there is always a chance that it will be one of the old, extra good varieties, such as 'St Brigid' or 'Ladham's Variety', or particularly good forms of *H. n. macranthus** (*H. n. altifolius**). I have half a dozen separate plantings of seedlings or small divisions of *H. niger*, which I am assured are something rather special.

I used to have two forms only of *H. foetidus*, our native plant, which has not a very good backbone and is best in a bare corner where its sprawlings are not too noticeable. The Italian form of *H. foetidus* is much more upright and a full-sized plant makes an imposing silhouette above double primroses or the silver and salmon-pink of *Lamium maculatum roseum**. I noticed a slightly different one in the Enfield garden of the late E. A. Bowles and learnt that that great gardener had collected it in the Roja valley. A friend gave me seedlings and now I have one or two good specimens under the shade of silver birch trees. This form has darker flowers, more delicately cut foliage with a suggestion of crimson in the stems. Another form comes from Mount Olympus and is taller and more slender in outline, and yet another I saw in a garden in Shropshire looks like a cross between *H. foetidus* and *H. orientalis*. I was given seed and shall be able to describe it better when I have lived with it.

H. foetidus is not a long-lived plant, but mercifully it usually seeds itself very generously, so there is usually a supply of young plants available when the old plants start to go brown and one by one the stems rot and have to be removed. I wonder if it is because it is so easy that it is by no means common. I find it most dramatic when in November and early December the pale green buds start to form above the dark, very well cut foliage. The top half of the plant is all pale green, stems, leaves and flower buds, and stands out in strong contrast to the dark green leaves. When the flowers eventually open and hang prettily with maroon edgings to the pale green flowers it is difficult to remember we are in mid-winter. Both this hellebore as well as *H. niger* and *H. corsicus** last very well as cut flowers.

The first time I lost a large plant of *H. corsicus** I felt as though I had lost a child and felt I must be to blame. That was many years ago and many plants of this hellebore have been in my life since. But now I know that they are just passing through, and not friends for life like the Lent Roses. The first year the Corsican hellebore flowers it will not be very big, and will have one or perhaps two trusses of its lovely apple-green flowers. The next year and the year after there will be more and after that it may start going back, and the gardener is edging in a new plant so that there will not be a gap in a year or two.

On its native stony hillsides the stems bearing the huge trusses of flowers do not attempt to stand upright but lie about on the ground, and in some woodland gardens the same thing happens, only here the stems make a complete circle round the new leaves springing up from the centre. It may be its natural way of growing but more than half the beauty of the plant is lost if it is allowed to lie about like this. I know the purists find something rather artificial about plants of *H. corsicus** neatly staked but I think it depends where and how you grow the plant. In the National Trust Garden, Tintinhull, in Somerset, the late Mrs Phyllis Reiss made this hellebore a feature of a shady border in one of her courts, and she staked her plants, which were quite big. At Bodnant in North Wales this hellebore is planted under trees in several parts of the garden but the plants I have seen there have always been young ones that do not need staking. The ones I grow under shady walls always need a little support when they get to the real flowering stage.

The evergreen foliage of *H. corsicus** is as beautiful and satisfying as that of *H. foetidus*, in light grey-green instead of dark green, netted with dark veins and scalloped at the edges.

Like most hellebores *H. corsicus** hangs its head until fertilised and then opens the flowers wide to the sky. The stamens are the first to go, then the nectaries, after that the floral segments disappear, leaving the seed pods standing up like a crown, heavy with swelling seeds.

The leaves of *H. lividus* are darker than those of *H. corsicus* and are more prominently veined. They have crimson on their undersides which is one way of telling if one has the true plant. The buds always seem to me to be more rounded than those of other hellebores, they are dove-coloured and open to flowers that are far from livid. I find it difficult to describe the colour for they have almost a mother o' pearl look, made by dull pink suffused over blue-green. It is not such a tough plant as the first two hellebores mentioned, which merely need to be anchored if they are planted in a position exposed to stormy winter wind. *H. lividus* really needs a sheltered corner and in very exposed gardens is sometimes grown in a cold greenhouse, and then it is discovered that the plant is sweetly scented.

Not everyone thinks that the small green-flowered *H. viridis* is worth growing because its flowers are the same colour as the leaves and not much bigger than an anemone. It is not quite evergreen for it disappears completely for about two months from late autumn until the new leaves appear in late February or early March. There is no mistaking them because they are smaller than most hellebores, almost fringed when they first appear, and very bright and shiny. The plant that grows wild in some parts of England, is, I understand, *H. viridis occidentalis**. There are several forms growing in Spain and other parts of the Continent and I have seen plants shown by nurseries as *H. viridis* which are very much paler in flower.

H. x *intermedius* (*H. torquatus*) is definitely one of the most rare of the hellebores, it is deciduous and seems to me to take its time before it decides to flower. I have several plants from different sources and so far not one has flowered for me although each year I get a leaf or two to raise my hopes and assure me that all is well down below and that with patience I shall get a flower some day. Again the colour is difficult to describe, a dull bluish mauve, almost grey, on the outside and green within, with a rim of the outside colour showing. The plant is deciduous and the leaves are rather like outstretched hands with slender fingers. The flower grows at right angles from its short stem and there is a suggestion of a white collar round its neck. Several nurseries sell *H.* x *intermedius**—at a high price—but I am not sure that all are authentic, in spite of the price.

The first hellebore to flower with me is *H. olympicus**, which I understand is the black hellebore recommended in old books for rejuvenating the aged. It is normally in bloom by October, with greenish white flowers, shading to green at the base. I am always trying to get seed and find that the first flowers are seldom any good for this but there is often a little from the later blooms.

December is the month the experts give for *H. atrorubens** to flower but some years the plum-purple flowers will open in early November. The plant is deciduous in its native Hungary but in our warmer climate the leaves persist almost to flowering time but they have usually gone when the first buds appear, at ground level. As stems grow more flowers open until the plant is about a foot high, with branching stems and several flowers, like a normal *H. orientalis*.

In November too the white buds of *H. kochii** are clustered at the base of the plant, all ready to open. This hellebore, which is the real *H. orientalis* and is also known as *H. caucasicus**, is easy to distinguish because of the very large leaves, in fresh green. The flowers are a greenish cream, about 3 in across, and when fully open are almost flat with wavy petals. The stems are seldom more than 15 in so it is a plant for a narrow bed or at the front of a helleborus planting.

H. odorus is another variety that usually opens before Christmas, though not till late December. The flowers are about 2 in across, rather rounded and a yellow-green. I never think the scent is sufficient to justify the name. It is a hands and knees job to discover it at all and then the faint suggestion of blackcurrant is hardly worth the trouble.

It will be a red letter day for me when *H. purpurascens* does at last flower for me. Very few people have this rare hellebore and I am lucky to have a plant. It was given to me as a seedling several years ago and every year I get leaves which persist longer than is usual with this deciduous plant. The flowers open when the stem is about an inch high and are rather small, the colour of a pigeon's breast on the outside and emerald-green inside. Eventually the stem may grow to about 8 in.

H. cyclophyllus is deciduous, and its new leaves always seem a long time coming through, often they do not appear till February and then one has to wait for the flowers, which are the last of the hellebores to open. They are large and a fairly deep green, hanging gracefully above the leaves. Some people swear that this hellebore is scented too, but if it is it must be very faint.

*H. abchasicus** is sometimes thought to be synonymous with *H. colchicus*, but the plants I have are much deeper in colour, almost maroon, with green markings and those of *H. colchicus* are a good medium pink.

There are many hellebores in January, *H. antiquorum** with greenish white flowers suffused with soft mauve-pink, *H. colchicus**, which has more and deeper pink on a paler ground, and *H. guttatus*, with large white or pale cream flowers, heavily spotted on the inside with shades of carmine and maroon.

There are innumerable unnamed hellebores and quite a number of good hybrids have been given names, but it would be quite impossible to sort them all back into their correct species. We know that any with spots inside have *guttatus* blood, and these include *H.* 'Hyperion', *H.* 'Lynton' and *H.* 'Prince Rupert'. The whites may have come from *H. orientalis* and among them are *H.* 'Albion Otto', *H.* 'White Swan' and *H.* 'White Ladies'. There are many in which pink predominates, 'Aurora' and 'Gloria', 'Apple Blossom', 'Peach Blossom' and 'Castile', and some of these are also heavily spotted inside the flowers.

Do the deep purples come from *H. atrorubens**, I wonder, or *H. abchasicus*? *H.* 'Apotheker Bogren' is a good purple and so is 'Combe Fishacre Purple'. *H.* 'Macbeth' is a rich colour but a poor doer, the darkest of all are *H.* 'Black Knight' and *H.* 'Ballard's Black'. Every season is exciting because the young plants coming into bloom may produce something really new. One with a picotee edge appeared in my garden one year, another which is mostly pink has rather long, drooping petals with a distinct wave. The best yellow I have seen is in the Myddelton House garden, and I gather it is lucky it is there at all. Towards the end of his life Mr Bowles had some visitors who badly wanted a bit of it and he generously told them to help themselves, which they did so liberally that there was practically nothing left. The nearest I have got to yellow is a very rich cream, Devonshire at its richest with a hint of green, but I cannot truthfully call it even pale yellow.

It is interesting to compare the balance of similarity in the hybrids made between species. *H. niger* and *H. corsicus** have produced *H.* x *nigricors**, and in the plants I have seen there is far more of *H. niger* in the hybrid and very little trace of *H. corsicus**, but *H. corsicus** predominates in *H. sternii**, which is

*H. corsicus** x *H. lividus*. There is a suggestion of pink in the flowers, and a trace of colour on the undersides of the leaves, but I do not think most people, who did not know, would think the plant was anything but *H. corsicus**. There is a hybrid called Bauer's, which I think came from the same cross, and there is very little difference in that either.

Though hellebores are primarily a winter flower some of them keep their flowers till the end of June, so there are very few months when there is not some interest in the hellebore world. Perhaps in time even this gap will be narrowed and we shall all envy the owners of gardens with enough shade to grow all the hellebores they want.

~ 16 ~
Hostas

While bergenias are good all-the-year plants, hostas are for summer enjoyment only and are best planted where their late autumn departure is not too obvious. At the end of the summer and in autumn the leaves of the hostas die down but they don't do it very prettily and the mass of decaying vegetation adds a dismal note to the drip of autumn rain. But one cannot do without hostas in any garden and certainly not in a shady one. Though they will grow in sun—and some experts claim that they flower better if planted in sun but their foliage is far lovelier when they are grown in shade—they are shade plants par excellence. I would not dream of planting any of mine anywhere but in shade and I find they flower extremely well and most of them set seed very generously. There is one that I do put at the edge of shade, *H. plantaginea*, which is the last to flower and is sometimes thought to need a little sun.

In America, where hostas are called plantain lilies, much work is being done in producing new ones. Many of the interesting ones were the result of crossing in a private back yard and some of these are finding their way to England. I had an unexpected payment and spent the money on two which have interesting variegation in the leaves and am now hoping to get some new breaks from the seed. Here we do not seem to be doing much about hybridising but rely on new ones that get here from Japan and America.

Some experts say that hostas do not like lime but I do not think this is so. They do not mind the heavy lime content in my soil and I know many limy gardens where they do extremely well. They do need plenty of humus, and are better if they get an occasional largesse of manure. A good place to grow them is under a north wall and they are lovely by the waterside as they like their shade to be moist. Given these requirements they are among the toughest plants I know, and do not seem to mind being lifted and divided any time that they are dormant. When people tell me they have lost their hostas I tell them to look again for those thick fleshy roots, like strong claws, which hold on with grim determination. It is not the kind of plant one digs up by mistake, and I do not think they often die, in fact, I think, they are amongst the most long-lived plants I know and put up with any amount of neglect.

Probably the most usually grown hosta is *H. ventricosa*, with medium green leaves. It is one of the easiest to grow and the smallest crown will make a brave showing. The flowers are darker lavender than most and are often veined with darker lines. The individual blooms are more rounded than many of the hostas, almost bell-shaped instead of looking like small trumpets.

The first to flower with me is *H. elata*, which has rather pale green heart-shaped leaves, ribbed and shiny, and flower stems almost 3 ft high. The lavender flowers are crowded together at the top of the stems and peter out as they go down, giving a rather thin effect.

The *H. fortunei* hybrids can have dark green or grey-green leaves, rather pointed and deeply grooved. The flowers are pale mauve and widely spaced on 18-in stems. It is a tough and reliable plant and wonderful for growing between shrubs where something generous and labour-saving is needed. It discourages all weeds and makes a lovely and colourful underplanting.

The most beautiful variety of *H. fortunei* is undoubtedly the one named *albopicta**, and I cannot think why, it is not white and though one could call its two-colour scheme painted, it has not the effect of paint splashed on a green background as some leaves have. Imagine the most delicate translucent golden-green with a darker green edging and you have this lovely hosta. To see it unfurling its leaves in spring is one of the greatest gardening thrills. I never know how the nurseries can provide those flawless vernal leaves for Chelsea, but I am always grateful that I can find refreshment in their clean, fresh loveliness after the onslaught of orange roses and bright salmon sweet peas. I love to see it bedewed after rain, and dread the end of summer when the leaves—like so many golden-foliaged plants—go green, although even then the darker green border round the leaves is quite distinct. I agree with the nurseries who put *aurea* after the *albopicta* in their catalogues, for the effect of this hosta is gold, not white. There is a form which is completely gold, I think it grows in the Savill Gardens, Windsor and I have seen it described as Windsor Gold. It is a more obvious plant than the delicate green-edged *albopicta** but it brings sunshine to a dull corner in the garden.

H. undulata* generally refers to the variegated plant, with wavy leaves in pale green heavily splashed with cream. This hosta could well be described as *albopicta** instead of one that bears that name. The flower stems are usually about 2 ft only and the flowers are medium violet. There is also an all-green undulated hosta, *H. u. erromena**, with smooth olive-green leaves. The flower stems can be as much as 3 ft with medium violet flowers.

I have a hosta with very large green leaves, very pointed and curved, which was given to me as *H. caerulea**. It has enormous leaves and tall flower stems with flowers a bluish lavender.

One of the best hostas to flower is the narrow-leaved *H. lancifolia*, an easy plant to please and one that increases well. The leaves are long and pointed and the flowers are soft lilac on 2-ft stems. They do not appear until September, when most of the other hostas are finished. A white-flowered white-edged form is one of the species I bought from America but it has not flowered for me yet. It is a small plant and does not seem to be quite so robust as the ordinary *H. lancifolia*.

There are several hostas with glaucous leaves and these are among the most beautiful of foliage plants and particularly lovely as an underplanting for old roses. *H. sieboldiana** is the name under which the glaucous-leaved hostas are usually found but sometimes they are given as *H. glauca* or *H. glauca robusta*. As a rule the leaves are wider and more heart-shaped than most of the hostas. The flowers are very pale blue, almost white, and the seed heads will last all through the winter and are a decorative feature of the winter garden, or they are pretty indoors in dried flower arrangements, with pearly transparent seed pods which open after the seeds have gone.

A form with rather wider, more pointed leaves and stumpy flower-heads, with a few leaves among the flowers, is known as *H. sieboldiana elegans**.

One of the biggest forms of the glaucous-leaved hosta is that grown at Kiftsgate Court, in Gloucestershire, with enormous leaves and near-white flowers. It has found its way into the nearby National Trust Garden, Hidcote, and looks lovely under the trees of the wild garden.

There is one neat and compact form which is associated with Crathes Castle in Scotland. Two forms with variegated leaves are probably sports of this plant. In one case the centres of the glaucous leaves are a bright greeny gold, and in the other (which is the second plant I got from America) the glaucous leaves have a wide edging of green-gold. Both these have pale lavender flowers.

The hostas with green leaves edged with white are not as a rule quite so robust and anxious to increase as most of the other kinds. The smallest is known as *H. albomarginata**. It never seems to me that it is a form of *H. lancifolia* as is sometimes suggested for the leaves are a little wider and more pointed and the rootstock is inclined to creep, which is not the case with *H. lancifolia*. The white margin on the leaves is very narrow and is hardly noticeable by the end of the summer.

In *H. crispula* the leaves are more variegated than margined because the white border on the slightly wavey-edged leaves is wider in some places than in others and much more distinct than in *H. albomarginata**. The leaves are as big as those of *H. fortunei*, in fact, the plant is sometimes known as *H. fortunei marginata-alba**. Its flowers are trumpet-shaped in pale lilac, growing in elegant spires.

There is another rather striking hosta with white-margined leaves which appears under several names. It was given to me as 'Thomas Hogg' and is not as big in leaf as *H. crispula* but is a bigger plant than *H. albomarginata**, with broader leaves. It is sometimes known as *H. sparsa*, but I understand should be called *H. decorata marginata** if one is to be correct. It is a Japanese plant, and there is a green form, *H. decorata normalis**.

The smallest hosta of all, *H. tardiflora*, is sometimes called *H. lancifolia tardiflora*, although its leaves are half the size of those of *H. lancifolia* and the flowers are crowded on 6-in stems. It is the only hosta I grow which I have felt is not quite happy with me, in fact I lifted one of my plants and replanted it in greensand, which is my panacea for all ailing treasures, but I cannot say that it ramps even there.

It is usually recommended to plant the white-flowered *H. plantaginea* in sun, no doubt because it flowers so late and needs a warm position to hasten its flowering, but it does quite well in shade. This is the last hosta to flower and it is always a toss-up whether the flowers will be able to get themselves open before early frosts mar their pure beauty. The foliage of this hosta is very beautiful and makes a patch of very pale green which one enjoys all through the summer but tempered with anxiety lest the leafy buds will be spoilt by the frost before they have time to open. Very often one watches the buds for weeks before they open and then a sudden frost may swoop down and kill them. And even if they flower it is rare for them to set seed. The flower-heads are rather tightly packed, with pale green leaves among the flowers; when they do flower they are so lovely that I walk that way many times a day to enjoy them and smell their delicious lily fragrance.

~ 17 ~

Variegations

It is not everybody who likes variegated plants, and those of us who do usually take a little time to become variegated addicts. I know I lost many opportunities of getting interesting variegated plants when I first started gardening because then I had not fallen under their spell. I had a great gardening friend who loved them and in those days I could never understand her passion.

Now I chase them just as fervently as anyone, partly from collector's avarice and also because they add so much to the general garden effect. In a shady garden they are particularly useful, bringing light to dark corners and showing up well against a dark background. And there are many that can be grown in shade. Roughly speaking those with silver variegation do better in shade and the golden-variegated plants usually like to be in sun. But there are exceptions, such as the golden-variegated form of *Iris pallida* which likes shade, and the golden-variegated ivies. I have *Hedera helix* 'Jubilee' up a shady wall and though its normal leaves are golden surrounded with dark green in this position many of them are pure gold. One would think the little golden ivy 'Buttercup' would like to sit in the sun but I have seen it making a lovely golden garland under the shade of trees.

All the variegated grasses do just as well in shade as sun. The tall and handsome miscanthus has several variegated forms. In *M. sinensis variegatus** the leaves are handsomely striped with white for the whole length, and in *M. s. zebrinus** the leaves have horizontal golden bands all the way up the stems.

Gardener's Garters or Ribbon Grass (*Phalaris arundinacea picta**) is an old-fashioned plant which increases with great freedom, and is attractive in any shady corner, particularly with purple-leaved shrubs such as the purple filbert, *Corylus maxima atropurpurea**, *Berberis thunbergii atropurpurea** or purple rhus, *R. cotinus atropurpurea**. It is usually more attractive if it is cut down early so that it makes a carpet of pale green and white, but on the other hand the 3-ft grassy stems turn quite white at the end of the season and remain so all through the winter. I plant this grass in large drainpipes sunk in the ground, otherwise it overruns other plants and is a tough customer to discourage.

The dwarf bulbous rooted grass, *Arrhenatherum elatius bulbosum variegatum**, makes a thick mat in a shady place but is not at all happy in sun. Another dwarf, *Holcus lanatus albo-variegatus**, is also happiest in shade. The slender *Molinia caerulea variegata** is a lovely little plant for growing in a spot where its attractive silhouette shows up. The tall variegated grasses and rushes are magnificent anywhere, the running *Glyceria aquatica variegata**, which delights in a damp spot, and *Stipa calamagrostis variegata**, which has lovely shades of bright red in its young growth.

Mounds of variegated foliage are most attractive under shrubs. The variegated apple mint, *Mentha rotundifolia variegata**, gives the greatest contrast for the deeper the shade the whiter it is. Even the golden-variegated mint, *M.* x *gentilis aurea**, known as ginger mint, does just as well in shade, but it runs more than most mints. The leaves of the variegated horehound, *Marrubium vulgare variegata**, have a speckled variegation but it spreads well during the season and in a mass is a soft pale green.

There are two variegated border phloxes which are best grown in shade. The variegated form of *P.* 'Border Gem' is the larger and tougher, and has a suspicion of pink in the white and silver of its leaves. *P.* 'Norah Leigh' is much more delicate in colouring, in fact, it is often almost white, and needs (with me at any rate) a great deal of care. But it is worth the trouble. It has pale lavender flowers and can be increased by cuttings, or division if one's clumps are big enough. The small variegated form of the rock phlox, *P. subulata*, is pretty and so is the variegated rock rose, *Helianthemum* 'Jubilee'.

Variegated ground cover plants look particularly well under shrubs and dark places. My standby is a yellow dead-nettle, *Lamium galeobdolon variegatum**, which grows most generously, looks nice always and is particularly beautiful in the winter when its silver and grey-green leaves are startlingly brilliant. None of the recipients of this plant have complained about it and I have had none of the hard looks that usually come after my donations of alpine strawberries, for instance. This lamium sends out long trails and makes roots at each leaf axil. It roots in gravel, in the poorest soil and at the edge of stones. As well as using it as a carpet to cover daffodils under silver birch trees, and to pour down a shady bank like a waterfall, I put pieces at the edges of paths where they meet walls or buildings, and which are favourite places for flourishing colonies of weeds. It has a great idea of artistry without any help from me and can transform a dark underplanting of ivy or claytonia by weaving its shining leaves among the dark ones but disturbing no one.

If I did not know *L. galeobdolon* I should recommend most highly *L. maculatum*, and I still do when something neater and more mat-like is better. While *L. galeobdolon* flings itself about, draping the ugly as it goes, *L. maculatum* merely spreads, and it flowers all the time, particularly well in winter, whereas *L. galeobdolon* flowers once only, in the spring (although it is not for its pale yellow flowers that I grow it). The commonest of the forms of *L. maculatum* is the one that flowers best, as usually happens, but those magenta-pink flowers are better than nothing when there are few flowers about. The pink form, *L. m. roseum**, has delightful salmon-pink flowers, without a touch of magenta, and there is also a beautiful white form.

Variegated periwinkles are just as prolific as the green ones, and look their best growing among plain green ones, and the variegated bugle, in shades of cream, pale green and a suggestion of pink, makes a delightful and delicate relief from darker plants. It is smaller and less robust than the other types. *Nepeta hederacea variegata** is another good ground cover for pale contrast, and the variegated form of pachysandra has paler leaves edged with silver.

There may be several variegated geraniums, I have two only so far, but there is always the chance that variegations may occur in one's own garden. I was given the variegated form of *G. macrorrhizum*, which is more cream than green and grows slowly. The variegated *G. punctatum** occurred in my own garden and I am grateful that the variegation has persisted. I have often found dandelions with variegated leaves, sometimes a primrose, and once a horseradish, but it was a fleeting change in each case.

The best of the variegated irises is without question *I. foetidissima variegata** which is at its best in the winter and at its whitest in the deepest shade. There is very little to see of the variegated forms of *I. pallida* in winter time, *I. japonica* is good if the weather is mild and its position sheltered, and *I. pseudacorus*, of course, turns green at the end of the summer. The variegated form of *I. laevigata* too waits for spring to make beautiful leaves. I think all these irises do best in shade; all have silver variegations with the exception of the golden-variegated form of *I. pallida*, and that is most definitely a plant for shade.

The most useful variegated plants are the evergreen ones, *Scrophularia aquatica**, for instance, and the symphytums. The variegated alpine strawberry keeps its leaves but so far I have not found a way to make it increase very fast. The variegated bramble is lovely in leaf; but one has only bare stems in winter, and the variegated form of *Artemisia vulgaris* does not make much contribution to the winter scene. This is another of the 'speckled' forms of variegation and looks its best before full grown. It is one of the plants I cut down early because its variegated habit is more marked in the young growth. Rue, on the other hand, is evergreen, and all that is necessary in autumn is to cut off the flowering stems and straggling branches, but it should be cut back hard in April. Cuttings of this plant which are variegated to begin with sometimes lose their variegation at time of rooting but go back as they grow on.

Everyone who has allowed it in the garden knows how honesty seeds itself. Variegated honesty, *Lunaria annua variegata**, is no exception but not all the children are well marked with white and much weeding out is required. So far the variegated nasturtium, *Tropaeolum major nanum**, 'Queen of Tom Thumb', has not perpetuated itself, but seed is easily obtainable.

One of the most spectacular variegated plants I know is variegated sedum and there seem to be several forms. I have been given *S. fabaria variegata**, *S. telephium roseo-variegatum**, which is the biggest, and ordinary variegated *S. spectabile**. They all look very much alike to me although I try to discover differences, and in fact *S. fabaria* is thought to be a sub-species of *S. telephium*, if not actually a synonym for it. They are easily increased by division or leaf cuttings and care has to be taken that all stems that revert to green are removed.

The variegated form of *Veronica gentianoides* is a good ground cover plant or for a patch at the front of a shady border. The foliage is dark and shiny and there are touches of pink as well as cream in the variegation. To keep the rosettes a good size they should be replanted singly each year. The same applies to the golden-variegated 'London Pride', but here one divides for increase rather than size, because the rosettes are usually quite big anyhow.

When the little blue-flowered *Liriope graminifolia** becomes variegated and has white instead of blue flowers it becomes an othiopogon and enjoys a special spot in the shade. This Chinese plant is evergreen, and so is *Reineckia carnea*, which sometimes produces variegated leaves in the midst of its green ones, leaves which I remove carefully with their roots to replant in a place where I hope they will increase.

At a glance it would seem that there are more variegated shrubs than herbaceous plants, and I realise that I have already mentioned a shrub among the plants for it is difficult to remember that vinca is classed as a shrub although to the normal person it does not appear to differ in any way from many herbaceous plants. Probably one could muddle some of the euonymus family in the same way. The attractive *Euonymus radicans**, for instance, is not a very shrubby plant in its early stages. This, in its variegated form of *E. r.* 'Silver Queen', is one of the best of the tribe, it will climb or crawl, sometimes it produces delicate pale pink fruits and its tough evergreen leaves never seem to be incommoded by the weather.

From there we can go down or up, down to the tiny *Euonymus buxifolius*, which is a slow-growing pygmy less than a foot high, with tiny silver-margined green leaves, or up to the bigger *E. japonicus* which has at least two forms. The most brilliantly variegated is *E. japonicus argenteo variegatus**, which has rounded leaves looking as though they had been splashed with cream paint. The less brilliantly marked spindle is *E. japonicus macrophyllus albus** (*latifolius variegatus*) which is very pleasant if the other is not around.

There are at least two forms of variegated box, and both do very well in shade. The neatest is *Buxus sempervirens elegantissima**, a small rounded bush like a plum pudding, which grows very slowly and can be put in the smallest garden. I grow mine near the house where the planting is low and because it is a pleasant sight in the winter, when many things look miserable, while it remains plump and complacent without a leaf out of place. The other has the same leaves but a more upright habit of growth, with branching stems and also suitable for a small garden. I was given a cutting and have never had a name for it, but it may be *B. s. latifolia*.

The two common variegated daphnes are the scented and early *D. odora marginata** which makes a spreading bush (and is strangely hardier than the green-leaved form) and variegated *Daphne cneorum*, which has gold-margined leaves. Both of these are evergreen but *D. mezereum*, which is deciduous occasionally produces seedlings with heavily variegated leaves. I am guarding a small variegated seedling at the moment and have to watch it carefully to see it does not vanish or go back to green.

In *Buddleia davidii* 'Royal Red' we have a plant that gives us the best of two worlds, for the flowers are among the richest of the buddleias and the cream-variegated leaves are very striking. It grows well and quickly as do all the buddleias and though it came first from a branch sport it has not reverted to green in my garden. Another exciting variegated tree is the variegated poplar, *Populus candicans* 'Aurora', which grows more slowly than the average poplar and is quite happy in the shade of taller trees. Its leaves are beautifully marked with pink and cream when young and last well in water. To get good colouring in the early growth it needs hard winter pruning. I did not do this the first year I had mine and feared the worst when the leaves remained green till July.

Hollies grow well in shade and the variegated forms are no exception. They can be margined with gold or silver, with broad or narrow leaves, and look well under a dark canopy provided by taller trees. They grow tall in time but the hedgehog holly, *Ilex aquifolium ferox**, grows more slowly and can safely be introduced into a small garden. The usual form is *I. a. f. aurea**, with gold variegations, but the silver-variegated type, *I. a. f. argentea**, is well worth seeking. They make compact little bushes which give all-the-year satisfaction.

There are several dwarf variegated shrubs which are good for growing in mixed borders where their delicate leaves mix well with the flowers and add pleasant interest. *Diervilla florida variegata** is about 3 ft high and has rather a spreading habit of growth and its pink flowers and white and pale grey-green leaves are very pretty. Another is the variegated form of the single *Kerria japonica*, *K. japonica variegata**. It seldom exceeds 2 to 3 ft in height and has an informal spreading habit, quite different from the stiff and upright double kerria. The single flowers are paler and much more pleasing, and grow on arching stems.

Griselinia littoralis is not hardy in many districts but it does well by the sea, making a sturdy bush with glossy leaves in apple green. The variegated form has very distinct white markings on the leaves. All the snowberries grow well in shade and the golden-variegated one, *Symphoricarpos orbiculatus variegatus**, is no exception. It does not have large berries like the others but in some years it is hung with tiny crimson fruits which give it its name of 'Coral Berry' or 'Indian Currant'; more often the berries are more like red beads and small ones at that. But the soft green foliage, netted with gold, is good among the flowers. The bush is never very tall and I cut mine down to about a foot each spring. It does not run like the common snowberry but it makes layers which can be severed to make new shrubs.

It is a pity that the most beautiful of the variegated veronicas (or hebes, as the shrubby veronicas are now called), are not hardy. *Hebe elliptica variegata** is the hardiest and though it has pleasant cream variegations it is not nearly so beautiful as *H. andersonii variegata**, which has larger leaves variegated with white and tinges of pink, and makes a large bush in mild districts but is best treated on a yearly cutting basis elsewhere. *H. speciosa variegata** is smaller and again not hardy. The form grown in the Edinburgh Botanic Garden has tinges of pink in the soft green and pale cream of its leaves.

Golden privet, *Ligustrum ovalifolium aureum**, is another exception to the rule that plants with golden foliage should be grown in full sun. It will grow in sun but it is even better in shade where it looks richer. This is a shrub that can be delightful, grown as a single specimen to bring sunshine to a shady border or trained up a north wall, but can be garish grown in a mass in full sun, perhaps as hedges to red brick council houses, as one sometimes sees it. *Ligustrum lucidum aureo variegatum** is not so often seen. It has leaves margined and mottled with strong yellow and pale cream. *L. lucidum tricolor** is the loveliest of all, with its green leaves bordered thickly with white, which often has a pinkish tinge in its early stages. It grows even more slowly than golden privet.

'Innocence' is the name of the variegated philadelphus. Its leaves have a deep cream variegation and it is a plant that must be grown in shade. One of the neatest and most attractive variegated shrubs is *Rhamnus alaternus variegata**. It is evergreen and has silver-grey and white foliage. Although not absolutely hardy everywhere, it has gone through some very severe winters with me without showing any signs of distress. It is slow growing and although it will eventually reach 6 ft it takes a long time.

Although *Cornus kousa* dislikes the lime in my soil the dogwoods with variegated leaves are luckily more tolerant. *C. alba sibirica variegata** has white markings on grey-green, while in *C. alba spaethii* there is much more gold in its leaves and stems that are conspicuously red in winter, making it a dual-purpose plant. *C. mas variegata** is almost triple-purpose for after enjoying silver-variegated leaves all through the summer there are tiny spidery flowers on the stems in February and March, which are followed by red cherry-like fruit. Two cornuses which are useful to grow under trees are C. *alternifolia variegata** and C. *controversa variegata**. Both have upright stems from which wide horizontal branches grow. Both have white and silver-green foliage but in C. *controversa variegata** it is heavier and the tree is bigger.

When the variegation is tricolor the effect is even better. Both the variegated fuchsias have this pleasing variegation which makes them specially attractive when growing over a wall or on a bank. F. *magellanica gracilis versicolor** is not so large and sprawling as some of the fuchsias and with its leaves variegated with silver and touched with pink, and its purple and carmine flowers it is a pretty little plant for intimate corners. F. *magellanica riccartonii** is a larger plant and in the variegated version there is more pink in the leaves, giving a somewhat crimson effect. Both these fuchsias grow well under trees and so does the tricolor St John's Wort. *Hypericum* x *moserianum* has a low and rather spreading habit which makes it useful for growing under shrubs or even tall perennials, almost ground cover in fact. The leaves are a symphony of white, pink and green shading to crimson at the edges.

It is not everyone who would take the risk of inviting *Polygonum cuspidatum** into the garden, although it has the most startling leaves in variegation. They are exciting from the moment they push through the soil, pointed like lobster claws and even brighter in colour. The colour is repeated as the leaves open and disclose splashes of cream and green as well. Of course the plant runs, in the way of polygonums, but in this case each wandering shoot is cherished because I know that from it will come up another vivid shoot. There is another polygonum with the same colouring but a much less stalwart habit. P. *filiforme variegatum** grows to about a foot with me and can be increased by cuttings.

We all know that jasmines do well on a north wall and those with variegated leaves are no exception. The most beautiful is a form of J. *officinale* variegated with white and tinged with pink, which is very delicate and finely cut. The golden-variegated jasmine is not attractive, unless I have a very bad form. It has rather strong-growing bright green leaves and the occasional splashes of bright yellow give rather a piebald effect. In J. *nudicaule* there is not enough gold to make it look as if it was really meant to be variegated. The variegated honeysuckle, on the other hand, *Lonicera japonica aureoreticulata**, has dull green leaves netted with fine golden lines, and mottled with pink in summer.

The variegated form of *Coronilla glauca* is beautiful as any variegated plant I have, with pale leaves heavily splashed with light cream. But it is not quite hardy and needs a sheltered spot. I know one that grows well on a south wall, shadowed and protected by an east wall at right angles. One of the pleasant traits of the coronillas is that they produce their yellow flowers in the winter.

Plant-name Changes

In her writings Margery Fish naturally used the plant names that were familiar to her and were considered acceptable at the time. But times have changed, and while many of the names she used are still current, and many that are not are nevertheless recognisable, some have changed completely.

So to help contemporary gardeners understand exactly which plants Mrs Fish is discussing, we have asterisked within the text all the names that have changed and listed these with the current accepted name below.

In some cases Mrs Fish gives two different names for the same plant, yet modern thinking may apply these two names to two different entities. She may also give two different names for what she asserts are two different plants yet modern thinking assures us that the two plants are the same. In some cases she indicates that one name has been superceded by another while it may now be clear that the first name, or another name altogether, is actually correct.

So while acknowledging that a full and accurate explanation of these nomenclatural niceties would be impossibly cumbersome, we hope that our simple listing will prove helpful. In identifying the correct names we sought advice and clarification from *The PlantFinder*, a range of modern encyclopedias and monographs together with expert individuals. However, because Mrs Fish grew such an extraordinary range of plants, some obscure even by today's standards and some now completely lost, a few minor problems remain unresolved.

In general we have changed Mrs Fish's original text as little as possible but the accepted manner in which names are styled in type has also changed over the years. So in some cases we have simply modified the expression of an otherwise correct name in order to avoid unnecessary additions.

The science of plant nomenclature perhaps should be, but is certainly not, a precise one; however we feel sure that by making these additions we add to an appreciation of Mrs Fish's writing and of the plants she grew.

Plant name in the text	Correct current name
Achillea *sibirica* 'Perry's White'	Achillea *ptarmica* 'Perry's White'
Achillea *sibirica* 'W. B. Child'	Achillea *ageratum* 'W. B. Childs'
Aconitum anglicum	Aconitum napellus Anglicum Group
Aconitum fischeri	Aconitum carmichaelii
Aconitum napellus bicolor	Aconitum x cammarum 'Bicolor'
Aconitum napellus carneum	Aconitum napellus subsp. *vulgare* 'Carneum'
Aconitum *wilsonii*	Aconitum Wilsonii Group
Adenophera potanini	Adenophora potaninii
Ampelopsis heterophylla	Ampelopsis glandulosa var. *heterophylla*
Amsonia salicifolia	Amsonia tabernaemontana var. *salicifolia*
Anaphalis margaritacea yedoensis	Helichrysum margaritacea var. *yedoensis*
Anemone blanda atrocaerulea	Anemone blanda 'Atrocaerulea'
Anemone blanda scythinica	Anemone blanda var. *scythinica*
Anemone huphensis elegans	Anemone x hybrida 'Elegans'
Anemone japonica	Anemone x hybrida
Anemone nemorosa allenii	Anemone nemorosa 'Allenii'
Anemone nemorosa robinsoniana	Anemone nemorosa 'Robinsoniana'
Anemone obtusiloba patula	Anemone obtusifolia var. *patula*
Anemone ranunculoides superba	Anemone ranunculoides 'Superba'
Anemone vitifolia robustissima	Anemone tomentosa 'Robustissima'
Aquilegia bertolinii	Aquilegia bertolonii
Aquilegia coccinea	Aquilegia 'Mrs Scott-Elliot's Strain'
Aquilegia vulgaris nivea	Aquilegia vulgaris 'Nivea' ('Munstead White')
Arabis albida rosa-bella	Arabis x arendsii 'Rosabella'
Arabis muralis	Arabis collina
Arnebia echioides	Arnebia pulchra
Arrhenatherum elatius bulbosum variegatum	Arrhenatherum elatius subsp. *bulbosum* 'Variegatum'
Artemisia lanata	Artemisia caucasica
Arum italicum marmoratum	Arum italicum 'Marmoratum'
Aruncus sylvester	Aruncus dioicus
Arundinaria auricoma	Pleioblastus auricomus
Arundinaria japonica	Pseudosasa japonica
Arundinaria murielae	Fargesia murieliae

Arundinaria nitida	Fargesia nitida
Asperula gussonii	Asperula gussonei
Asperula lilaciflora caespitosa	Asperula lilaciflora
Aster cordifolius elegans	Aster cordifolius 'Elegans'
Aster diffusus horizontalis	Aster lateriflorus 'Horizontalis'
Aster tradescantii	Aster pilosus var. demotus
Astilbe chinensis pumila	Astilbe chinensis var. pumila
Atriplex hortensis cupreata	Atriplex hortensis 'Copper Plume'
Begonia evansiana	Begonia grandis subsp. evansiana
Bellevallia romanus	Bellevallia romana
Belladonna hybrids	Belladonna Group
Berberis stenophylla	Berberis x stenophylla
Berberis thunbergii atropurpurea	Berberis hunbergii f. atropurpurea
Bergenia 'Ballawley Hybrid'	Bergenia 'Ballawley'
Bergenia beesiana	Bergenia purpurascens
Bergenia cordifolia orbicularis	Bergenia x schmidtii
Bergenia delavayi	Bergenia purpurascens var. delavayi
Bergenia ligulata	Bergenia ciliata f. ligulata
Bergenia milesii	Bergenia stracheyi
Bergenia stracheyi milesii	Bergenia stracheyi
Brodiae laxa	Triteleia laxa
Buxus sempervirens elegantissima	Buxus sempervirens 'Elegantissima'
Calceolaria polyrrhiza	Calceolaria polyrhiza
Caltha palustris alba	Caltha palustris var. alba
Caltha polypetala	Caltha palustris var. palustris
Campanula burghaltii	Campunula 'Burghaltii'
Campanula glomerata acaulis	Campanula glomerata var. acaulis
Campanula glomerata alba	Campanula glomerata var. alba
Campanula glomerata dahurica	Campanula glomerata var. dahurica
Campanula glomerata superba	Campanula glomerata 'Superba'
Campanula grandis	Campanula persicifolia subsp. sessiliflora
Campanula isophylla mayi	Campanula isophylla 'Mayi'
Campanula latifolia macrantha	Campanula latifolia var. macrantha
Campanula planiflora alba	Campanula persicifolia var. planiflora f. alba
Campanula planiflora caerulea	Campanula persicifolia var. planiflora
Campanula x stansfieldii	Campanula 'Stansfieldii'
Campanula x van houttei	Campanula x 'Van-Houtei'
Cautlea lutea	Cautleya gracilis

Cautlea robusta	Cautleya spicata 'Robusta'
Caphalaria tatarica	Cephalaria gigantea
Cerinthe aspera	Cerinthe glabra
Clematis calycina	Clematis cirrhosa var. balearica
Clematis flammula rubro marginata	Clematis x triternata
Clematis orientalis	Clematis tibetana subsp. vernayi
Clematis tangutica 'Gravetye'	Clematis tangutica 'Gravetye Variety'
Colchicum autumnale album	Colchicum autumnale 'Album'
Colchicum autumnale minus	Colchicum autumnale var. minor
Colchicum speciosum album	Colchicum speciosum 'Album'
Colchicum speciosum rubrum	Colchicum speciosum 'Rubrum'
Cornus alba sibirica variegata	Cornus alba 'Sibirica Variegata'
Cornus alba spaethii	Cornus alba 'Spaethii'
Cornus alba 'Westonbirt'	Cornus alba 'Sibirica'
Cornus alternifolia variegata	Cornus alternifolia 'Argentea'
Cornus controversa variegata	Cornus controversa 'Variegata'
Cornus mas variegata	Cornus mas 'Variegata'
Cortaderia argentea carminea rendatleri	Cortaderia argentea 'Rendatleri'
Cortaderia argentea pumila	Cortaderia selloana 'Pumila'
Corylus maxima atropurpurea	Corylus maxima 'Purpurea'
Cotoneaster lactea	Cotoneaster lacteus
Crocus tomasinianus	Crocus tommasinianus
Cyananthus integer	Cyananthus microphyllus
Cyclamen europaeum	Cyclamen purpurascens
Cyclamen neapolitanum	Cyclamen hederifolium
Cyclamen neapolitanum album	Cyclamen neapolitanum 'Album'
Cyclamen orbiculatum	Cyclamen coum
Cyclamen pseud-ibericum	Cyclamen pseudibericum
Cydonia japonica alba	Cydonia x superba 'Alba'
Cydonia lagenaria moerloesii	Cydonia speciosa ''Moerloosei'
Cydonia 'Snow'	Cydonia speciosa 'Snow'
Cydonia x superba simonii	Cydonia speciosa 'Simonii'
Daphne odora marginata	Daphne odora 'Aureomarginata'
Daphne cneorum eximia	Daphne cneorum 'Eximea'
Daphne collina	Daphne sericea Collina Group
Daphne retusa	Daphne tangutica Retusa Group
Deutzia kalminiflora	Deutzia x kalminiflora
Deutzia x rosea campanulata	Deutzia x rosea 'Campanulata'
Dicentra eximia alba	Dicentra eximia 'Snowdrift'

Diervilla florida variegata	Weigela 'Florida Variegata'
Disporum oreganum	Disporum hookeri var. oreganum
Dracocephalum prattii	Nepeta pratti
Elaeagnus pungens aureo-variegata	Elaeagnus pungens 'Maculata'
Elaeagnus pungens dicksonii	Elaeagnus pungens 'Dicksonii'
Embothrium lanceolatum	Embothrium coccineum Lanceolatum Group
Endymion hispanicus	Hyacinthoides hispanica
Erigeron mucronatus	Erigeron karvinskianus
Erinus 'Dr Hanele'	Erinus alpinus 'Dr Hähnle'
Erythronium revolutum 'White Beauty'	Erythronium californicum 'White Beauty'
Escallonia 'Apple Blossom'	
Escallonia x edinensis	Escallonia x 'Edinensis'
Escallonia iveyi	Escallonia 'Iveyi'
Euonymus japonicus argenteo variegatus	Euonymus japonicus 'Ovatus Aureus'
Euonymus japanicus macrophyllus albus	Euonymus japonicus 'Latifolius Albomarginatus'
Euonymus radicans	Euonymus fortunei
Euphorbia amygdaloides rubra	Euphorbia amygdaloides 'Purpurea'
Euphorbia amygdaloides superba	Euphorbia amygdaloides 'Superba'
Euphorbia amygdaloides variegata	Euphorbia amygdaloides 'Variegata'
Euphorbia androsaemifolia	Euphorbia esula
Euphorbia biglandulosa	Euphorbia rigida
Euphorbia characias	Euphorbia characias subsp. characias
Euphorbia epithymoides	Euphorbia polychroma
Euphorbia pilosa major	Euphorbia polychroma 'Major'
Euphorbia robbiae	Euphorbia amygdaloides var. robbiae
Euphorbia sibthorpii	Euphorbia characias subsp. wulfenii var. sibthorpii
Euphorbia valde-villoscarpa	Euphorbia villosa subsp. valdevilloscarpa
Euphorbia wulfenii	Euphorbia characias subsp. wulfenii
Fatshedera x lizei	x Fatshedera lizei
Filipendula hexapetala flore plena	Filipendula hexapetala 'Multiplex'
Filipendula rubra venusta	Filipendula rubra 'Venusta'
Forsythia suspensa pallida	Forsythia suspensa 'Pallida'
Fritillaria verticillata thunbergii	Fritillaria thunbergii
Fuchsia magellanica gracilis versicolor	Fuchsia magellanica 'Versicolor'
Fuchsia magellanica riccartonii	Fuchsia magellanica 'Riccartonii'
Galanthus elwesii whittallii	Galanthus elwesii var. whittallii

Galanthus nivalis cilicicus	Galanthus nivalis subsp. cilicicus
Galanthus nivalis corcyrensis	Galanthus reginae-olgae subsp. corcyrensis
Galanthus nivalis flavescens	Galanthus nivalis 'Sandersii'
Galanthus nivalis lutescens	Galanthus nivalis 'Sandersii'
Galanthus nivalis reginae-olgae	Galanthus reginae-olgae
Galanthus nivalis scharlokii	Galanthus nivalis 'Scharlockii'
Galanthus nivalis virescens	Galanthus nivalis 'Virescens'
Galanthus nivalis viridapicis	Galanthus nivalis 'Viridapicis'
Gaulnettya 'Wisley Pearl'	Gaultheria x wisleyensis 'Wisley Pearl'
Gentiana lagodechiana	Gentiana septemfida var. lagodechiana
Gentiana macaulayi	Gentiana x macaulayi
Geranium alpinum	Geranium grandiflorum var. alpinum
Geranium anemonifolium	Geranium palmatum
Geranium atlanticum	Geranium malviflorum
Geranium endressii 'Wargrave'	Geranium x oxonianum 'Wargrave Pink'
Geranium endressii x G. striatum	Geranium endressii x G. versicolor
Geranium ibericum	Geranium x magnificum
Geranium pratense plenum violaceum	Geranium pratense 'Plenum Violaceum'
Geranium psilostemon	no longer known as G. armenum
Geranium punctatum	Geranium x monacense 'Muldoon'
Geranium sanguineum lancastriense	Geranium sanguineum var. striatum
Geranium striatum	Geranium versicolor
Geranium traversii 'Russell Pritchard'	Geranium x riversleaianum 'Russell Prichard'
Gladiolus byzantinus	Gladiolus communis subsp. byzantinus
Glyceria aquatica variegata	Glyceria maxima var. variegata
Haberlea rhodopensis virginalis	Haberlea rhodopensis 'Virginalis'
Hamamelis japonica zuccariniana	Hamamelis japonica 'Zuccariniana'
Hamamelis mollis brevipetala	Hamamelis mollis 'Brevipetala'
Hebe andersonii variegata	Hebe x andersonii 'Variegata'
Hebe elliptica variegata	Hebe x franciscana 'Variegata'
Hebe speciosa variegata	Hebe speciosa 'Variegata'
Hedera 'Curly Locks'	Hedera helix 'Curlilocks'
Hedera helix cristata	Hedera cristata 'Parsley Crested'
Hedera helix deltoidea	Hedera hibernica 'Deltoidea'
Hedera helix feastii	Hedera cristata 'Königer'
Hedera helix sagittaefolia	Hedera cristata 'Sagittifolia'
Hedera 'Silver Queen'	Hedera 'Tricolor'

Hedychium spicatum acuminatum	*Hedychium spicatum* var. *acuminatum*
Helichrysum angustifolium	*Helichrysum italicum*
Helichrysum serotinum	*Helichrysum italicum* subsp. *serotinum*
Helichrysum siculum	*Helichrysum stoechas* subsp. *barrelieri*
Helichrysum trilineatum	*Helichrysum splendidum*
Helleborus abchasicus	*Helleborus orientalis* subsp. *abchasicus*
Helleborus antiquorum	*Helleborus orientalis*
Helleborus atrorubens	*Helleborus* 'Early Purple'
Helleborus caucasicus	*Helleborus orientalis*
Helleborus colchicus	*Helleborus orientalis* subsp. *abchasicus*
Helleborus corsicus	*Helleborus argutifolius*
Helleborus cyclophyllus	*Helleborus* 'Cyclophyllus'
Helleborus dumetorum	*Helleborus* 'Dumetorum'
Helleborus guttatus	*Helleborus orientalis* subsp. *guttatus*
Helleborus intermedius	*Helleborus torquatus*
Helleborus x intermedius	*Helleborus torquatus*
Helleborus kochii	*Helleborus orientalis*
Helleborus niger altifolius	*Helleborus niger* 'Maximus'
Helleborus niger macranthus	*Helleborus niger* subsp. *macranthus*
Helleborus x nigricors	*Helleborus nigercors*
Helleborus olympicus	*Helleborus orientalis*
Helleborus orientalis (kochii)	*Helleborus orientalis*
Helleborus purpurascens	*Helleborus* 'Purpurascens'
Helleborus sternii	*Helleborus x sternii*
Helleborus viridis occidentalis	*Helleborus viridis* subsp. *occidentalis*
Hepatica x ballardii	*Hepatica x media* 'Ballardi'
Hepatica lilacina	*Hepatica transsilvanica* 'Lilacina'
Hepatica triloba	*Hepatica nobilis*
Heuchera x tirelloides	x *Heucherella tiarelloides*
Holcus lanatus albo-variegatus	*Holcus mollis* 'Variegatus'
Hosta albomarginata	*Hosta fortunei* 'Albomarginata'
Hosta albopicta	*Hosta* var. *albopicta*
Hosta caerulea	*Hosta ventricosa* 'Caerulea'
Hosta decorata marginata	*Hosta decorata* var. *decorata*
Hosta decorata normalis	*Hosta decorata* var. *normalis*
Hosta fortunei marginata-alba	*Hosta fortunei* 'Marginata Alba'
Hosta sieboldiana	*Hosta* 'Sieboldiana'
Hosta sieboldiana elegans	*Hosta sieboldiana* var. *elegans*
Hosta undulata	*Hosta* 'Undulata'

Hosta undulata erromena	*Hosta undulata* var. *erromena*
Hyacinthus amethystinus	*Brimeura amethystina*
Hydrangea integerrima	*Hydrangea serratifolia*
Hydrangea involucrata hortensis	*Hydrangea involucrata* 'Hortensis'
Hydrangea petiolaris	*Hydrangea anomala* subsp. *petiolaris*
Hydrangea sargentiana	*Hydrangea aspera* subsp. *sargentiana*
Hydrangea villosa	*Hydrangea aspera* Villosa Group
Hylomecon japonicum	*Hylomecon japonica*
Hypsella longiflora	*Hypsella reniformis*
Ilex aquifolium ferox	*Ilex aquifolium* 'Ferox'
Ilex aquifolium ferox argentea	*Ilex aquifolium* 'Ferox Argentea'
Ilex aquifolium ferox aurea	*Ilex aquifolium* 'Ferox Aurea'
Iris foetidissima variegata	*Iris foetidissima* 'Variegata'
Iris laevigata 'Rose Queen'	*Iris ensata* 'Rose Queen'
Iris ochraurea	*Iris* 'Ochraurea'
Iris ochroleuca	*Iris orientalis*
Iris 'Snow Queen'	*Iris sanguinea* 'Snow Queen'
Kalmiopsis	*Kalmiopsis leachiana*
Kentranthus macrosiphon	*Centranthus macrosiphon*
Kerria japonica variegata	*Kerria japonica* 'Variegata'
Lamium galeobdolon variegatum	*Lamium galeodolon* 'Variegatum'
Lamium maculatum roseum	*Lamium maculatum* 'Roseum'
Lathyrus vernus albo-roseus	*Lathyrus vernus* 'Alboroseus'
Layia elegans	*Layia platyglossa*
Leonotis leonurus	*Leonurus ocymifolia*
Leucojum aestivum 'Gravetye'	*Leucojum aestivum* 'Gravetye Giant'
Leucojum vernum carpathicum	*Leucojum vernum* var. *carpathicum*
Leucojum vernum wagneri	*Leucojum vernum* var. *vagneri*
Ligularia clivorum	*Ligularia dentata*
Ligustrum lucidum aureo variegatum	*Ligustrum lucidum* 'Aureovariegatum'
Ligustrum lucidum tricolor	*Ligustrum lucidum* 'Tricolor'
Ligustrum ovalifolium aureum	*Ligustrum ovalifolium* 'Aureum'
Linaria aequitriloba	*Cymbalaria aequitriloba*
Linaria 'Canon J. Went'	*Linaria purpurea* 'Canon Went'
Liriope graminifolia	*Liriope muscari*
Lithospermum diffusum 'Grace Ward'	*Lithodora diffusa* 'Grace Ward'
Lithospermum diffusum 'Heavenly Blue'	*Lithodora diffusa* 'Heavenly Blue'
Lithospermum purpureo-caeruleum	*Buglossoides purpureocaeruleum*
Lobelia vedrariensis	*Lobelia* x *gerardii* 'Vedrariensis'

Lonicera grata	Lonicera x americana
Lonicera japonica aureoreticulata	Lonicera japonica 'Aureareticulata'
Lonicera japonica halliana	Lonicera japonica 'Halliana'
Lonicera periclymenum belgica	Lonicera periclymenum 'Belgica'
Lonicera periclymenum serotina	Lonicera periclymenum 'Serotina'
Lonicera tellmanniana	Lonicera x tellmanniana
Lunaria annua alba	Lunaria annua var. albiflora
Lunaria annua variegata	Lunaria annua 'Variegata'
Lychnis dioica fl. pl.	Silene dioica 'Flore Pleno'
Lysichitum americanum	Lysichiton americanus
Lysichitum camtschatcense	Lysichiton camtschatcensis
Lysimachia ciliosa	Lysimachia ciliata
Lysimachia nummularia aurea	Lysimachia nummularia 'Aurea'
Macleaya cordata 'Coral Plume'	Macleaya cordata 'Kelway's Coral Plume'
Magnolia lennei	Magnolia x soulangeana 'Lennei'
Magnolia nigra	Magnolia liliflora 'Nigra'
Magnolia sinensis	Magnolia sieboldii var. sinensis
Magnolia soulangeana	Magnolia x soulangeana
Mahonia aquifolium undulata	Mahonia x wagneri 'Undulata'
Marrubium vulgare variegata	Marrubium vulgare 'Variegata'
Mentha x gentilis aurea	Mentha x gracilis 'Variegata'
Mentha rotundifolia variegata	Mentha suaveolens 'Variegata'
Milium effusum aureum	Milium effusum 'Aureum'
Mimulus cupreus 'Red Emperor'	Mimulus 'Red Emperor'
Mimulus luteus duplex	Mimulus luteus 'Duplex'
Miscanthus sinensis variegatus	Miscanthus sinensis 'Variegatus'
Miscanthus sinensis zebrinus	Miscanthus sinensis 'Zebrinus'
Molinia caerulea variegata	Molinia caerulea 'Variegata'
Muscari azureum album	Muscari azureum 'Album'
Muscari comosum monstrosum	Muscari comosum 'Plumosum'
Muscari moschatum flavum	Muscari macrocarpum
Muscari paradoxum	Bellevallia paradoxa
Muscari racemosum	Muscari neglectum
Mutisia retusa	Mutisia spinosa var. pulchella
Narcissus x mini-cycla	Narcissus x 'Minicycla'
Narcissus nanus	Narcissus minor
Neillia longiracemosa	Neillia thibetica
Nepeta hederacea variegata	Glechoma hederacea 'Variegata'

Nepeta 'Souvenir d'André Chaudron'	*Nepeta sibirica* 'Souvenir d'André Chaudron'
Olearia gunniana	*Olearia phlogopappa* (A.M. form)
Orchis maculata	*Dactylorhiza maculata*
Origanum vulgare aureum	*Origanum vulgare* 'Aureum'
Oxalis rosea	*Oxalis rubra*
Paeonia ludlowii	*Paeonia mascula* var. *russoi*
Paeonia lutea ludlowii	*Paeonia delavayi* var. *ludlowii*
Paeonia obovata alba	*Paeonia obovata* var. *alba*
Paeonia peregrina 'Sunshine'	*Paeonia peregrina* 'Otto Froebel'
Paeonia russii	*Paeonia mascula* var. *russoi*
Parthenocissus trifoliata	*Parthenocissus tricuspidata*
Peltiphyllum peltatum	*Darmera peltata*
Pennisetum caudatum	*Pennisetum alopecuroides*
Pennisetum caudatum ruppellii	*Pennisetum setaceum*
Phalaris arundinacea picta	*Phalaris arundinacea* 'Picta'
Philadelphus coronarius aureus	*Philadelphus coronarius* 'Aureus'
Phlox divaricarta laphamii	*Phlox divaricarta* subsp. *laphamii*
Phormium tenax alpinum	*Phormium tenax* 'Alpinum'
Phormium tenax purpureum	*Phormium tenax* 'Purpureum'
Phormium tenax variegatum	*Phormium tenax* 'Variegatum'
Phormium tenax veitchii	*Phormium tenax* 'Veitchianum'
Phyllitis scolopendrium	*Asplenium scolopendrium*
Pieris forrestii	*Pieris formosa* var. *forrestii*
Platycodon grandiflorus apoyama	*Platycodon grandiflorus* 'Apoyama'
Polemonium coeruleum	*Polemonium caeruleum*
Polygala purpurea	*Polygala chamaebuxus* var. *grandiflora*
Polygonum affine	*Persicaria affinis*
Polygonum amplexicaule	*Persicaria amplexicaulis*
Polygonum bistorta superbum	*Persicaria bistorta* 'Superba'
Polygonum campanulatum	*Persicaria campanulata*
Polygonum cuspidatum	*Fallopia japonica*
Polygonum cuspidatum compactum	*Fallopia japonica* var. *compacta* (female form)
Polygonum filiforme variegatum	*Persicaria virginiana* 'Variegata'
Polygonum paniculatum	*Polygonum molle*
Polygonum reynoutria	*Fallopia japonica* var. *compacta*
Polygonum tenuicaule	*Persicaria tenuicaulis*
Polygonum vacciniifolium	*Persicaria vaccinifolia*

Polystichum angulare	Polystichum setiferum
Pratia treadwellii	Pratia angulata 'Treadwellii'
Primula altaica	Primula vulgaris subsp. sibthorpii
Primula bhutanica	Primula whitei 'Sherriff's Variety'
Primula denticulata cachemiriana	Primula denticulata var. cachemiriana
Primula helodoxa	Primula prolifera
Primula x pubescens alba	Primula x pubescens 'Alba'
Pyracantha coccinea lalandei	Pyracantha coccinea 'Lalandei'
Pyrancantha fructo-luteo	Pyracantha 'Fructo-luteo'
Pyrancantha rogersiana flava	Pyracantha rogersiana 'Flava'
Ramonda myconi rosea	Ramonda myconi 'Rosea'
Ranunculus acris fl. pl.	Ranunculus acris 'Flore Pleno'
Ranunculus speciosus plena	Ranunculus constantinopolitanus 'Plenus'
Rhamnus alaternus variegata	Rhamnus alaternus
Rhazya orientalis	Amsonia orientalis
Rhus cotinus atropurpurea	Cotinus coggygria Rubrifolius Group
Rodgersia pinnata superba	Rodgersia pinnata 'Superba'
Rodgersia tabularis	Astilboides tabularis
Rosa 'Dr Van Fleet'	Rosa 'Dr W. Van Fleet'
Rosa viridiflora	Rosa x odorata 'Viridiflora'
Rudbeckia speciosa	Rudbeckia fulgida var. speciosa
Salix alba argentea	Salix alba var. sericea
Salix matsudana tortuosa	Salix babylonica var. pekinensis 'Tortuosa'
Salix vitellina pendula	Salix alba 'Tristis'
Santolina incana	Santolina chamecyparissus
Santolina neapolitana	Santolina pinnata subsp. neapolitana
Sarcocca humilis	Sarcococca hookeriana var. humilis
Saxifraga cordifolia	Saxifraga 'Cordifolia'
Saxifraga umbrosa 'Elliott's Variety'	Saxifraga umbrosa 'Clarence Elliott'
Saxifraga umbrosa 'Geum'	Saxifraga x geum
Saxifraga umbrosa melvillei	Saxifraga umbrosa 'Melvillei'
Saxifraga umbrosa variegata	Saxifraga umbrosa 'Variegata'
Schizophragma integrifolia	Schizophragma integrifolium
Scilla hispanica	Hyacinthoides hispanica
Scilla sibirica	Scilla siberica
Scilla tubergeniana	Scilla mischtschenkoana
Scrophularia aquatica	Scrophularia auriculata
Sedum fabaria variegata	Sedum fabaria 'Variegata'
Sedum spectabile	Sedum alboroseum 'Mediovariegatum'

Sedum telephium roseo-variegatum	Sedum telephium 'Roseovariegatum'
Senecio greyi	Brachyglottis 'Sunshine'
Senecio tanguticus	Sinacalia tangutica
Skimmia foremannii	Skimmia foremannii 'Veitchii'
Solidago 'Lemore'	x Solidaster luteus 'Lemore'
Solidaster luteus	x Solidaster luteus
Spiraea 'Anthony Waterer Improved'	Spiraea 'Anthony Waterer'
Spiraea arguta	Spiraea 'Arguta'
Spiraea prunifolia plena	Spiraea prunifolia
Stipa calamagrostis variegata	Stipa calamagrostis 'Variegata'
Stranvaesia davidiana	Photinia davidiana
Symphoricarpos albus laevigatus	Symphoricarpus albus var. laevigatus
Symphoricarpos orbiculatus variegatus	Symphoricarpos orbiculatus 'Foliis Variegatis'
Symphytum peregrinum	Symphytum x uplandicum
Symphytum tauricum	Symphytum orientale
Symplocos crataegoides	Symplococus paniculata
Thalictrum dipterocarpum	Thalictrum delavayi
Thalictrum minus	Thalictrum minus 'Adiantifolium'
Thalictrum speciosissimum	Thalictrum flavum subsp. glaucum
Tradescantia 'J. C. Wegulin'	Tradescantia x andersoniana 'J.C. Wegulin'
Tricuspidaria lanceolata	Crinodendron hookerianum
Trollius 'Brynes Giant'	Trollius 'Bryne's Giant'
Tropaeolum major nanum	Tropaeolum majus 'Alaska'
Tropaeolum 'Queen of Tom Thumb Mixed'	Tropaeolum 'Alaska'
Tropaeolum 'Queen of T.T. Ryburgh Perfection'	Tropaeolum 'Fire and Ice'
Veronica teucrium trehane	Veronica prostrata 'Trehane'
Veronica virginica	Veronicastrum virginicum
Viburnum burkwoodii	Viburnum x burkwoodii
Viburnum foetans	Viburnum grandiflorum f. foetans
Viburnum fragrans	Viburnum farreri grandiflorum
Viburnum opulus xanthocarpum	Viburnum opulus 'Xanthocarpum'
Viburnum tomentosum plicatum	Viburnum plicatum f. tomentosum
Viburnum tomentosum plicatum grandiflorum	Viburnum plicatum 'Grandiflorum'
Viola 'Bowles Black'	Viola tricolor 'Bowles Black'

Index

B

C

D

daffodil 47
   see also Narcissus
daisy *see Bellis*
damp shade, plants for 57-64
Danae racemosa 38
Daphne
   D. blagayana 35, 73
   D. x burkwoodi 35
   D. cneorum 35, 118
     *D.c. eximia** 35-6, 73
   *D. collina** 35
   D. laureola 35
   D. mezereum 35, 118
     D.m. grandiflora alba 35
   *D. odora marginata** 118
   D. pontica 35
   *D. retusa** 36
   D. 'Somerset' 35
   D. tangutica 35
day lily 22-3
   see also Hemerocallis
Delphinium 15-16
   D. 'Azure Fairy' 15
   D. tatsienense 15
Deutzia
   D. x elegantissima 38
   *D. kalminiflora** 38
   *D. x rosea campanulata** 38
Dianella
   D. intermeda 84
   D. tasmanica 84
Dicentra
   *D. eximia alba** 70
   D. formosa 70
     D.f. 'Bountiful' 70
   D. spectabilis 11
*Diervilla florida variegata** 118
*Disporum oreganum** 84
dog's tooth violet *see Erythronium dens-canis*
dogwood *see Cornus*
Doronicum 45
   D. austriacum 11
   D. 'Miss Mason' 11
*Dracocephalum prattii** 19

E

Echinacea 'The King' 19
Elaeagnus pungens
   E.p. aureo-variegata 92
   *E.p. dicksonii** 92
elder 45
elm trees 44
*Embrothrium lanceolatum** 32
*Endymion hispanicus** 42, 50
enkianthus 32
Epigaea
   E. asiatica 32
   E. repens 32
Erica
   E. carnea 39
     E.c. 'Springwood White' 39
   E. darleyensis 39
   E. mediterranea 39
*Erigeron mucronatus** 91
Erinus 'Dr Hanele'* 91
Erysimum perofskianum 75
Erythronium
   E. californicum 48
   E. dens-canis 42, 47
     E.d. 'Franz Hals' 48
     E.d. 'Pink Perfection' 47
     E.d. 'Rose Beauty' 47
     E.d. 'Snowflake' 47
   E. grandiflorum 48
   E. revolutum 48
     *E.r. 'White Beauty'** 48
   E. tuolumnense 48
Escallonia
   E. 'Apple Blossom' 89
   *E. x edinensis** 89
   *E. iveyi** 89
Euonymus
   E. alatus 37
   E. buxifolius 117
   E. europaeus 37, 45
   E. hamiltonianus 37
   E. japonicus 117
     *E.j. argenteo variegatus** 117
     *E.j. macrophyllus albus** 117
   E. latifolius variegatus 117

H

Haberlea rhodopensis 71
  *H. r. virginalis** 71
Hacquetia epipactis 11
Hamamelis
  *H. japonica zuccariniana** 31
  H. mollis 31
    *H.m. brevipetala** 31
  H. 'Ruby Glow' 31
hart's tongue fern *see Phyllitis scolopendrium**
heathers 39
Hebe
  *H. andersonii variegata** 119
  H. cupressoides 38-9
  *H. elliptica variegata** 119
  *H. speciosa variegata** 119
Hedera
  H. 'Buttercup' 114
  H. canariensis 88
  *H. 'Curly Locks'** 88
  H. 'Glacier' 88
  H. 'Gloire de Marengo' 88
  H. 'Green Ripple' 88
  H. helix
    *H.h. cristata** 88
    *H.h. deltoidea** 88
    *H.h. feastii** 88
    H.h. 'Jubilee' 88, 114
    *H.h. sagittaefolia** 88
  H. 'Silver Queen' 88
Hedychium
  H. densiflorum 79
  H. gardnerianum 80
  *H. spicatum acuminatum** 79-80
Helianthemum 'Jubilee' 115
Helichrysum
  *H. angustifolium** 93
  *H. serotinum** 93
  *H. siculum** 93
  *H. trilineatum** 93
Helleborus 9, 10, 18, 43, 104-9
  *H. abchasicus** 108
  H. 'Albion Otto' 108
  *H. antiquorum** 108

H. 'Apotheker Bogren' 108
H. 'Apple Blossom' 108
*H. atrorubens** 10, 104, 107, 108
H. 'Aurora' 108
H. 'Ballard's Black' 104, 108
H. 'Bauer's Hybrid' 109
H. 'Black Knight' 104, 108
H. 'Castile' 108
*H. caucasicus** 107
*H. colchicus** 108
H. 'Combe Fishacre Purple' 108
*H. corsicus** 10, 105-6, 108-109
*H. cyclophyllus** 104, 108
*H. dumetorum** 104
H. foetidus 10, 105
H. 'Gloria' 108
*H. guttatus** 104, 108
H. 'Hyperion' 108
*H. intermedius** 104, 107
*H. kochii** 107
H. 'Ladham's Variety' 105
H. lividus 106, 109
H. 'Lynton' 108
H. 'Macbeth' 108
H. niger 10, 104-5, 108
  *H.n. altifolius (maximus)** 10
  *H.n. macranthus** 105
*H. x nigricors** 108
H. odorus 107-8
*H. olympicus** 10, 107
H. orientalis 10, 107
H. 'Peach Blossom' 108
H. 'Potter's Wheel' 10, 105
H. 'Prince Rupert' 108
*H. purpurascens** 104, 107
H. 'St Brigid' 105
*H. sternii** 108
H. torquatus 107
H. viridis 104, 106-7
  *H.v. occidentalis** 107
H. 'White Ladies' 108
H. 'White Swan' 108
propagation 104
situations 10, 104
Hemerocallis
  H. citrina 22
  H. fulva 22

M

O

P